# BEFORE SAYING "YES" TO MARRIAGE . . .

## *101 Questions to Ask Yourself*

**Sidney J. Smith** WITHDRAWN

Published by:
Sidney James Publishing Company
115 East Mission Street
Santa Barbara, CA 93101

**Publisher's Cataloging-in-Publication**

*(Provided by Quality Books, Inc.)*

Smith, Sidney J.
    Before saying "yes" to marriage— : 101 questions
to ask yourself / Sidney J. Smith. —
1st ed.
    p. cm.
    Includes bibliographical references.
    ISBN: 0-9671329-1-6
    1. Mate selection.  2. Marriage.  3. Marriage
compatibility tests.  I. Title.

HQ801.S65 1999                          646.7'7
                                        QBI99-844

Printed in the United States of America

# A TRULY HAPPY MARRIAGE INCLUDES LOTS OF HUGGIN' AND KISSIN'

## A Note to the Reader

Since the book is addressed to men and women, I used feminine and masculine pronouns alternatively. I hope this format makes both female and male readers feel personally included.

## Disclaimer

The author of this book is not a marriage counselor, and the ideas contained herein may conflict with mainstream opinion. The advice regarding premarital matters outlined in this book may not be suitable for everyone. The publisher and/or author disclaim any liability, loss, or risk incurred directly or indirectly as a result of the use or application of any of the contents of this book.

# Contents

# Introduction

The honeymoon is over when you wake up one morning and ask yourself, "Is this all there is to marriage?" And then a few years down the line you think to yourself, "That's not the person I *thought* I married. He seemed so wonderful when we first met. What happened?" Perhaps you wonder to yourself, "I thought the person I married was different from the others I've been involved with. It's taken me all this time to see that I married the wrong person. Will I EVER have the opportunity to find Mr./Ms. Right?"

If the above scenarios seem familiar to you or if you have some concerns about your prospective marriage partner, this book is for you. There are many reasons why couples get the prenuptial jitters; many have them even as they walk down the proverbial aisle. Usually it's because they don't know each other as well as they should and it's difficult to anticipate any potential problems. So why not take a step in the right direction and ask each other the questions found in this book before you say "yes" to marriage.

My wife, Madeline, and I have experienced a combined 108 years of married life (54 years for her and 50 for me with our first mates, plus our 4 years together). In both our previous successful marriages and in our present one together, we've learned a lot of lessons. We're pleased to offer our combined insights into what makes a marriage work to those of you who are venturing into this life of sharing and caring. The intent of this book is to make you aware of what you should know about each other before getting married.

This book is a tool for all those considering marriage, regardless of age or ethnic background. It raises many important questions for you to think about and talk over with your future partner. Some of these questions will apply to your situation and way of life while others may not. Still, if only one question raises a red flag that needs to be explored by the two of you, this book will have served its purpose.

Marriage is a sacred rite of passage where two people promise to share their lives together. If your experience in life is limited, you may not know what this really means. This book will provide you with a starting point. Take the time to review the questions offered here and make individual lists of those questions you feel need to be discussed jointly.

It's better to recognize your differences before marriage than after. If you find there are questions you can't resolve, consider meeting with a marriage counselor or a trusted friend who has your welfare in mind. If major differences can't be resolved, you may want to reconsider your decision. A marriage ceremony is brief compared to the long, drawn-out process of divorce. Don't rush into marriage without committing yourself to the idea that your love for each other will prevail, regardless of problems that may arise in the future. Sharing your life with the one you love is one of God's greatest gifts, and a successful marriage is the reward you'll receive for doing your homework before you get married.

Enjoy the experience of true love and appreciation for that special someone in your life.

*"A happy marriage turns lights on, not only in your house but in your heart."*

**—Sidney J. Smith**

# Planning Your Future Together

Contemplating marriage is the beginning of a wonderful adventure. Marriage itself is a challenging experience, one that takes you to places you wouldn't arrive at as a single person. Since you're reading this book, I assume that you're leaning in the direction of getting married and that you have dreams and aspirations for that marriage. Dreams are important, and I encourage you to DREAM BIG. However, keep in mind that at some point reality will kick in. Whether you expect it to or not is another matter. Eventually, reality will make its grand entrance, especially when it comes to the day-to-day experiences of living together. For now, though, let's just discuss your DREAMS and your DESIRES.

A marriage without dreams and goals is a marriage without direction. Exploring each other's cherished dreams and burning desires for your future together can be enlightening, or sometimes a totally unexpected revelation! For example, you may have dreams of traveling the world and never settling down in one place, whereas your future spouse may think that going a hundred miles down the freeway to Disneyland is an exciting once-in-a-lifetime trip (and possibly the only one he plans to take). Can you meet somewhere in between regarding each other's expectations? For instance, could you both agree to a once-a-year vacation in some enchanting hideaway?

Dreams allow even the most humble person to live momentarily in a world full of riches. Dreams become even more exciting when they include sharing them with a loving partner. Setting goals and sharing dreams that are acceptable and important to both of you are important steps BEFORE and AFTER taking your marriage vows; it binds you together and ensures that your commitment will last. Explore each other's dreams for the future and see if you can combine them in a way that satisfies both of you. Make your marriage a lifelong voyage navigating the uncharted waters of your dreams and discovering the true happiness that is waiting for you wherever you make port together. And may ALL your dreams come true!

# Are You Considering Living Together before Marriage?

In today's world, living together before marriage is generally accepted, whereas not too many generations ago it was considered immoral. Why the change in attitude? One answer is the sexual revolution of the 1970s. Now, however, the ideas regarding premarital sex and living together prior to marriage are somewhat different. Couples feel that it's important to get to know each other very well before marrying so there won't be any surprises. They want to make sure they're choosing the right partner before making a final commitment. Others think it's a good way to get some of the benefits of marriage and avoid the chance of divorce. But then there are those for whom such an arrangement is forbidden by their own personal or religious beliefs.

A recent report based on extensive research, published by The National Marriage Project, estimates that "over half of all first marriages are now preceded by cohabitation, compared to none earlier in this century." It further indicates that "living together before marriage increases the risk of breaking up after marriage." Therefore, it's not a good tryout for marriage. While offering a few principles that may help young adults who have never been married achieve long-lasting marriages, the report advises couples to not live together at all before marriage or limit cohabitation to the shortest possible period of time.

If you're thinking about living together before marriage, you might find it helpful to discuss the questions in this book before moving in together, just as couples are doing who are in the process of planning their wedding. It might be less complicated financially to end an unmarried relationship, but the emotional scars still linger if you split up from this kind of an arrangement. Why put yourself needlessly in a situation like this without talking about some of the issues posed in this book? Your future will be affected by the decisions you make today, so make every effort to be sure they're the right ones.

 **Sid's Wisdom:** Talk to friends who lived together before they got married and those who didn't. Listen and consider the pros and cons of each. With this information in hand, the ultimate choice will be yours.

# For What GOOD Reasons Are You Getting Married?

It's amazing how many different reasons people give for getting married. They range from "All my friends are married" to "Marriage is something I've always dreamed of" to "I need someone to share my rent and other expenses." No kidding! That's why this is such an important question to ask not only of yourself but of each other. Also, there has to be a more practical answer than what most couples respond—"Why are we getting married? Because we're in love!" Although falling in love is an important ingredient, it shouldn't be the only one.

Life presents many challenges, and despite all the excitement of being able to tell your closest friends and fellow workers that you're going to be married, choosing the right person to spend the rest of your life with is one of the most important decisions you'll ever make. If you live in a culture where marriages are arranged by the parents, you don't have to make a choice at all. It's done for you. Surprisingly, the commitment to a lifelong relationship in arranged marriages is as successful as the commitment of partners who choose themselves. Could it be that the parents know something about their offspring that the offspring may not know about themselves? Surely you've known couples who have fallen in love but aren't really right for each other. They might really believe they are, but their family and friends foresee trouble on the horizon. I often wonder why family and friends don't speak up. Nevertheless, everyone is relieved when the flaws in the relationship begin to show up and the couple decides to call it quits BEFORE walking down the aisle.

Courtship is quite different from actually being married. When you're "in love," it's easy to think that when problems arise, you'll just work it out. Make a list of all the reasons you have for getting married. Communicate the mental picture you have of your future marriage to your fiancé. Be specific. Ask your future spouse, "What role do you think a husband or wife should take?" Other questions in this book may also help you visualize your marriage of the future. Add to your list some of your common goals. Having an openness about these issues, as well as a good visual image, can help bring success to your lifetime relationship.

**Sid's Wisdom:** Don't be afraid to ask each other's family and friends if they have reservations about your marriage. If they do, ask for specifics and consider them carefully. Talk them over with your prospective marriage partner to determine how valid they are. Only in the movies do the words "If any man can show why this couple may not lawfully be joined together, let him now speak, or else forever hold his peace" get a real live response from the audience.

# Do You Have Goals in Life That You Think May Be Thwarted by Marriage?

When you come face to face with the prospect of getting married, the goals you've set for yourself may come into conflict with marital responsibilities. Up until the moment you say "I do," you're an independent agent. But once you say those two words, you take on the new obligation of sharing your life with another person. Some of the goals you had as a single person may suddenly seem impossible to reach. Don't despair! You don't have to sacrifice them.

As a couple, if you can discuss and see the importance of each other's hopes and dreams, then you should be able to work together to make them come true. You may discover that some of your goals are not so different, and these then become combined goals within your marriage. Individual goals can often be easily carried out if you support each other's hopes and dreams. And then there's always the added joy of sharing in the success when your partner accomplishes something important.

**Sid's Wisdom:** There are many situations in life where one chooses to give up something in order to gain something of equal or greater value. This is very different from giving up something important to you. If this should result in resentment, then your marriage could really be in trouble.

# *Do You Have a Desire to Be Wealthy?*

Is a big house with a swimming pool and tennis court part of your game plan for the future? Do you want to send your children to private schools? Do you figure that after you're married, the two of you should have matching Ferraris? Are you and your partner in sync about such ambitions?

Sometimes couples get married without ever discussing the lifestyle they hope to have in the future. If you're the kind of person who works hard, but making money isn't a priority, you should make this known to your potential spouse. What if she's thinking, "Once we're married, he'll have to get a better job. He's going to have to afford me a better life." By committing to each other under these circumstances, you could be heading for disaster.

There's nothing wrong with wanting a comfortable and abundant life. Being successful in your work can give you and your spouse the freedom to pursue other interests and enjoy many years of happiness without financial concerns. However, keep in mind that money alone can't buy happiness. There are many other ingredients that lead to a happy marriage.

 **Sid's Wisdom:** Even lottery winners are not assured happiness in their marriages. Many such couples divorce after becoming winners. When it comes to marriage, keep your eye on the final reward: a long and loving relationship.

# Are You Both Happy about Where You'll Be Living?

For many couples, the thought of settling into a first residence together is exciting and full of creative opportunities. For others, it can be a hair-raising experience, particularly if it involves one partner having to pick up and relocate.

Right off, speak up if you think you're not going to be happy where you'll be living. Job location primarily determines this, so sometimes it's just a matter of getting adjusted to a new place. If this isn't the case, there are compromises that you can make. For example, perhaps one of you works in an office in the middle of a large city and the other person can't stand living in the city. Check out the surrounding areas. A short commute to work may save a lot of stress on your relationship.

If you're a woman planning to move into your future husband's existing home, you've probably already redesigned every room of the house in your mind. But have you let him in on all of this? It's probably better not to surprise him with a truckload of new furniture and wallpaper hangers in the living room when you return from your honeymoon. Get to know each other's tastes and the interior design changes you want to make before you start living together as man and wife. Many times, the man will leave this all up to his wife. However, I know of one woman who married an interior decorator and she wasn't allowed to change even the color of the sheets on their bed. Another friend was told by her future spouse that she could do whatever she wanted when it came to decorating their apartment. When the time came to move in together, however, he was adamant about keeping the hideous, gigantic, pink velvet sofa that he'd gotten as a bargain some years ago. She compromised, but it drove her nuts until he decided he'd better give it up.

As your marriage progresses, your tastes and living space needs will no doubt change. Perhaps a new job will require you to move, or maybe a newborn will enter your life and you'll need more space. Maybe you'll get tired of the high tech look of your decor and want to go shabby chic. In any case, you have a lot of time to experiment and try out new things. Take it slow, be open to each other's ideas, and enjoy the journey along the way.

 **Sid's Wisdom:** You can certainly dream of your rose-covered cottage, but be prepared to compromise when settling into your first home. Changes can take place over time.

# Do You Think You Could Live In a Foreign Country?

If you or your potential spouse is in an occupation that might include relocating to another country, are you open to starting a new life abroad? As romantic as it may seem, the adjustment to living in a foreign country could prove unsettling. You'd have to make new friends and perhaps learn a new language. With the world becoming smaller and smaller, a job opportunity abroad may not be too far-fetched. Whether or not you'd look at this as an exciting opportunity depends largely on how adventurous a person you are. It's one thing to travel the world as a visitor; it's quite another to become part of the fabric of another culture altogether.

If your spouse-to-be is originally from another country, is there a chance he might want to move back there? Years ago, a woman acquaintance met a man from another country. They both worked in the same industry and had similar values and the same religious background. In addition, they shared a lot of interests. It seemed like a match made in heaven. They married and had two children. As time went on, he found it difficult to find enough work in the United States to meet their needs. An opportunity presented itself in his native country to make a good living. They talked at length about moving there as a family unit. Unfortunately, she felt it would be too difficult to adapt herself to a new part of the world, and they eventually separated. It was a difficult decision on both their parts, but it was not something they had foreseen or spoken of before they were married. Had they been able to see ahead to this situation, they might have talked about it and decided not to marry or at least make some other compromises.

 **Sid's Wisdom:** An awareness of future predicaments can oftentimes, but not always, spare the heartache of an unwanted separation or divorce.

## *Will Your Marriage Be Strong Enough to Survive a Life-Threatening Experience?*

When you make the commitment to marry, you have a certain image of what that entails. You may visualize raising children, starting a family business, traveling after you retire, and eventually growing old gracefully together. However, many unexpected, unplanned events take place in a marriage. Some are happy and joyful, some are not. One of the most unfortunate things that can happen at any age is that one partner is diagnosed with a life-threatening illness and suddenly the other is faced with the possibility of losing his or her loved one. How would you deal with such a crisis? Are you prepared to set aside your dreams for the future and concentrate on the immediate needs of your partner?

It's difficult to predict exactly how one will react when faced with a situation like this, but we know it'll take inward strength to live through such an event. Does your potential spouse show promise in the area of character strength? So many things ensue that will affect both of you when tragedy strikes the homefront: changes in lifestyle will take place, financial problems present themselves, children and family members must be informed and then prepared for whatever might occur, and many other things as well.

In the face of adversity, when the commitment is strong between you, things that were planned for future years may suddenly seem less important and you can easily put them aside. You must be prepared to confront your immediate problems and face them together.

 **Sid's Wisdom:** Plan for the future, but be aware that life is always changing. Be flexible enough to be able to adjust to needed changes, often beyond your control. Dedication to supporting each other is your primary goal.

# Family Background

When two people who come from similar family backgrounds get married, they may have a much better union than a couple who come from very different backgrounds. Why is this? Simply because the first couple's relationship is made easier by all the customs and habits they're used to and share at the outset. They're more aware of each other's expectations because they were most likely raised by parents with similar values and child-rearing practices. In marriage, this couple will experience many unspoken agreements between them that create an important bond in their pledge to one another.

Two people who are from different backgrounds can have a successful marriage, too, but their relationship may suffer added stress because they'll have to make adjustments to each other and to each other's lifestyles that a couple coming from similar backgrounds won't have to make. They may need to build a solid base of common interests and define their roles in the household early on. And they'll have to either agree on or negotiate major and minor issues.

Ethnic, religious, cultural, and socioeconomic differences between families all require special consideration. These can affect everything from the way children are raised to the kind of food you eat, as well as to the type of furniture you decorate your home with. This is why it's important to share your family backgrounds and childhood memories before you say "I do." Be prepared for a give and take relationship. Everyone gains and no one really loses.

# How Many Siblings Do You Have?

If your potential spouse is an only child or a child from a large family, you could be either blessed or cursed. An only child often gets spoiled because there are no other siblings to receive the parents' attention. If an only child has parents who doted on him day and night, the chance of getting your needs met may be questionable. On the other hand, if the parents were loving and mindful of the way they raised their only child, then your future partner is possibly a better prospect for having been raised in a loving atmosphere.

As an adult, a spoiled child can be as demanding as he was when a child. The expectations are that life will continue under the new regime as it did prior to your marriage, having attention paid to his every need. If each of you is an only child, who gives in to whom? Hopefully, you should both have confidence that your marriage won't become a competitive arena wherein every decision becomes a battleground.

If your potential spouse is from a large family and didn't get the attention she needed from her parents, she may also have a hard time fulfilling your needs because she'll need a lot of attention herself. A therapist once told me that, contrary to the image we have of the happy flock in a large family, the children almost always suffer from lack of parental guidance and attention and shouldn't hesitate to go into therapy. On the other hand, someone raised in a large family may be very flexible and nurturing.

Adjusting to each other's lifestyle and needs calls for a fair amount of compassion. This can't be achieved with two stubborn individuals vying for attention. Compromise is the name of the game. If your partner is willing to listen to your needs and you to his, the passage to living together as a married couple can be satisfying and rewarding.

 **Sid's Wisdom:** Conflict is inevitable within a relationship, and it's a perfectly normal part of marriage. It's how you handle conflict that can make or break your union. Learning to compromise and work through your conflicts is essential to a healthy marriage.

# What Are Your Educational Backgrounds?

Educational diplomas are not always the measure of success in life. Life experiences and on-the-job training can also bring a good deal of knowledge to one's existence. However, as a couple you should find out if you have strong feelings about each other's educational backgrounds. For example, if your future wife has a college degree and you don't, do you feel unequal? If she has a higher paying job, do you feel inadequate or jealous?

Too great a difference in your educational backgrounds can spell trouble. Take a look at your prospective mate's family environment. Are there books in the household? Did the parents encourage reading and academic prowess? Would you be happy with a spouse who had never read a book in his life? How much intellectual stimulation do you think is essential for your relationship to be successful?

Bear in mind that there are many kinds of intelligence, and most people possess several different types. For example, some people think analytically while others base their thoughts more on how they feel. Some individuals retain a lot of facts easily and are great at crossword puzzles and trivia. Others are adept at assembling things and use their common sense to see things through to a conclusion. These talents may be gained through formal education or life experiences. However they're acquired, the sharing of such talents can be truly rewarding to the one sharing as well as the recipient.

 **Sid's Wisdom:** Check out each other's attitudes toward learning and creative expression. Personal growth should be an ongoing endeavor in one's life. By supporting each other in continual learning experiences and situations, both of you will benefit.

# Were Your Parents Good Role Models?

You're influenced by the example set by your parents in their marriage. If they had a happy marriage, then you're more inclined to look at marriage as a joyful experience. If your parents expressed their love for one another often, and they shared their love with you, then you'll probably act the same way with your spouse and children. If your parents have an unhappy marriage or are divorced, then you may be soured on marriage. Perhaps you both know a couple whose marriage you hold in high regard. If so, what is it about their marriage that appeals to you and what can you learn from them?

Do you know the marriage history of your loved one's parents? This could tell you a lot about how he may act in your own marriage. If your prospective mate's parents are divorced, talk about why they divorced and how it affected him. This could be the key to unlocking suppressed feelings that need to be understood before you enter into a lifelong partnership.

 **Sid's Wisdom:** Don't be shy about approaching your respective parents or friends and asking them what they consider to be the success, or failure, of their marriage.

# What Is the Medical History of Your Future Spouse's Family?

Before you enter into marriage, find out from your potential mate if there's any history of alcoholism, mental disorder, unexplainable illness, or other such conditions in his or her family. Any one of them could result in serious problems in your marriage. Ask about the drinking habits of the family and how serious illness, if any, was handled. Many couples avoid treading on this delicate ground beforehand because they're afraid of what they might learn. Even when you ask the questions, you might not get satisfactory answers and you may have to dig for the truth. But isn't it better to hear about it before taking your vows than after? In this way, you can become informed about these issues until you're more confident that they won't affect your marriage. Remember, the healthier you both are to begin with, the healthier your marriage will be. This means both physical and emotional health.

 **Sid's Wisdom:** If there's a history of physical or mental illness in your future mate's family, become as knowledgeable as possible about the condition. Discuss the circumstances with a psychologist or your medical doctor.

# Is There Any History of Physical or Mental Abuse in Your Respective Families?

If you or your potential mate comes from a home where physical or psychological abuse is a common occurrence, there's a good chance you or he will use violence in your own home. Make every effort to find out if he has these tendencies. Talk to those who know him best. Then try to see your prospective mate under different circumstances. Watch him around children and around the elderly. Expose him to your family and friends when you're not there. He could be on his best behavior around you and act differently when he's around others. Hopefully, you know your partner well enough to determine this isn't true, but it never hurts to have a second opinion.

A seemingly safe but temperamental person may get physically abusive only under certain circumstances. Insignificant things that didn't bother him when you dated might set him off once you're living together. Watch for outward signs of potential domestic violence. Some of the warning signs of an abusive person are: He has a violent temper; he strikes or throws things when he's angry; he makes you afraid; he fought at school and threatened his younger siblings; he says you caused him to get angry; he abuses pets; he wants to limit your power in the relationship, for example, he thinks you should get an allowance or you shouldn't work or go to school; he wants to limit your outside involvement; he thinks he should make all the big decisions; he puts you down or humiliates you. You may find yourself excusing his bad behavior and blaming yourself for doing something wrong.

**Sid's Wisdom:** If your potential spouse exhibits many of these characteristics, he needs therapy and you shouldn't marry until he's rehabilitated. You must remind yourself that abuse is inappropriate and you won't be a part of it. This applies to both sexes. And don't think that by marrying him you can change him. Despite your best intentions, that seldom works, and you may be putting yourself in a dangerous position.

*"Chains do not hold a marriage together. It is threads, hundreds of tiny threads which sew people together through the years. That is what makes a marriage last–more than passion or even sex!"*

—Simone Signoret

# Life Experiences

Generally speaking, the older you are, the more life experience you've had. This is true with respect to career, travel, world views, and other facets of life. If you're a young adult, you may not have experienced as much in your life as someone approaching midlife or older. The ability to maintain perspective during crises comes with age and experience. A mature person, regardless of age, tends to be more open and confident in his or her beliefs. As a result, everything is not necessarily black and white to those who have had a variety of experiences. There are shades of gray as well.

The amount and kinds of life experience you have had affects the way you respond to the world and the kind of people you're drawn to. For example, a person who spent time in the Peace Corps is not likely to have much in common with the yuppified Wall Street broker.

The importance of sharing your life experience with your potential mate can't be stressed enough. This is where you'll learn about each other's willingness toward ongoing personal growth. This is where you'll find out about your intended's hidden fears and secrets. This is where you'll find out if there's too wide a gap between you for a successful marriage. You may find it wise to postpone the marriage until these concerns are lovingly addressed and a mutual level of comfort is reached concerning your future together.

# If There's a Big Difference in Your Ages, Have You Considered the Potential Difficulties?

There is great allure for some men and women in finding a younger mate these days. The appeal of the older man–younger woman scenario may lie in the woman's desire to be married to a man of importance and means. For him, the attraction may have to do with having a young, beautiful woman on his arm for the whole world to admire. It's becoming more and more common to see the flipside of this arrangement—the older woman–younger man scenario. In this instance, the allure for the woman is often that it makes her feel youthful and vibrant again. For the younger man, there's often a mysterious charm to an older woman. Whichever the case may be, it's good to have a clear understanding of the reason for the attraction and whether it'll sustain a long-term relationship or it's just a way to bolster one's own ego.

Assuming that, as a couple with a big age difference, you have a deep and lasting love for one another, then it's important to think about when the age difference will really begin to make a difference (if it hasn't already!). If, for instance, when you marry you're twenty and he's forty-five (or vice versa), in twenty years one of you will be forty and the other sixty-five! Unless you're expecting to rediscover the ancient secrets of the fountain of youth, this could be a significant difference at this stage of the marriage. Remember, too, that a man in his sixties is still able to procreate, whereas a woman of the same age is presumably incapable of bearing children, if that's important.

You'll also want to be prepared to accept the attitudes of other people who may view you as misguided or perhaps even a little immoral. You know not to judge a couple merely by their age, but other people may not be so open-minded. Will it bother you to have others judge you this way? Will you be able to handle the fact that your friends and parents may not approve of your marriage? These are all important things to consider—even though age difference is not, and should not be, the determining factor for happiness within a marriage.

 **Sid's Wisdom:** Regardless of your age difference, always remember that ultimately the decision to marry must be yours and your partner's. No one else should try to influence you or make that decision for you.

## If Either You or Your Potential Spouse Has Been Married Before, How Do You Intend to Approach a Second Marriage?

It's unfortunate that all marriages aren't made in heaven. If you or your potential spouse has gone through the pain and agony of a divorce, you may be carrying a fair amount of baggage from your past disappointment into this new relationship. Hopefully, though, you're willing to let go of the sad and unhappy memories and will try not to allow your past experiences to cloud your future. It may help to share with each other the reasons that the first marriage failed. If you, in part, were personally responsible for the undoing of your first marriage, be prepared to make the necessary changes so that you won't make the same mistakes again. If your new intended mate is still on good terms with his or her former spouse, perhaps it would be possible to have a heart-to-heart talk with this person about why he or she feels the marriage didn't work out.

Statistics indicate that over half the divorced men and women remarry within two years after their divorce. Do you have children from the previous marriage who will be living with you? Have they been made aware of your plans to join in marriage? Have they expressed concerns about having a new mom or dad in their lives? Have you spent enough time with them to know if you'll enjoy being a parent to them? If your potential marriage partner admits to having a serious problem with your children, the problem won't disappear. For the sake of the children, get rid of any doubts beforehand. If you don't, yours probably will not be the happy family you're envisioning.

 **Sid's Wisdom:** Enter the prospect of a second marriage with an open mind and heart. After all, you're involved with a totally new and different person. Realize that time is in your favor. Allow for a period of adjustment.

# Do You Have Hidden Fears?

Inside all of us lurk fears—fears that even our closest friends and family members don't know about. People have a tendency to keep their fears hidden deep inside because they're afraid of what others might think of them. In some instances, they believe those concerns might reveal a side of them that others will consider silly, or unwarranted, and yet deep inside themselves they seem real.

Most people avoid their fears or situations that can cause anxiety. Try to get your significant other to name three things that cause him anxiety or to be fearful. What's the worse thing that could happen? For example, maybe the person you want to marry has fears about getting married and is afraid to tell you. If so, and you can get him to express these fears, try to narrow it down by having him complete this sentence: "What scares me the most about telling you my fear about getting married is _____." When you can be specific about your fears, you can confront them and start to overcome them. Hopefully, your new and caring partner will help you face your fears.

Fear can reveal itself in a variety of ways. Many people are afraid of change and will stay in a dead-end job simply because the unknown frightens them. They hesitate to take chances because they may fail. Perhaps as a child you were always afraid of the dark. Imagine the look on your loved one's face as you're about to spend your first night together in conjugal bliss and you refuse to turn out the lights. Get your fears out in the open and watch the shadows disappear.

 **Sid's Wisdom:** Ask each other to make a self-assessment of your greatest fears, then discuss them openly with each other.

# Is the House You're Planning to Move Into with Your Spouse a New Home or One He Once Shared with His Former Wife?

If you plan to marry someone who still lives in the house he and his previous wife lived in, you probably would expect him to move out and find a new home for the two of you. Why would you even consider moving into a house he shared with a former wife and having to deal with the ghost of his past marriage? Wouldn't he want to begin his new life with you without all the memories of life with his ex? However, there may be some valid reasons for keeping the house. It could be the location. Perhaps it's fully paid for, in which case a mortgage on a new house wouldn't be necessary, and the money you would save could pay for the children's education. Besides, you can always redecorate the house.

After my first wife died and I renewed my acquaintance with Madeline, I found myself in this very situation. Madeline, a long-time friend of my former wife, wasn't sure about living in the house where I had spent so many years with my first wife. I had hoped there wouldn't be a problem. It had been our family home for years and it was fully paid for. Now I was ready to begin my new life with Madeline and we agreed that she could redecorate to her heart's content. We listened to each other's concerns. Madeline, who had had a happy marriage and raised a family of her own, finally became comfortable with the idea of sharing the house with me. The final touch was when, during the redecorating, we decided to have an artist friend come in and paint a family mural on the ceiling and walls of our new exercise room. There, in full color, sharing the room with us, are our former spouses and all the children—and we love it. It unifies us as a family in a way nothing else could have.

 **Sid's Wisdom:** Look at all sides of your potential living situation. Be willing to negotiate, and get creative if you plan to share a home with beautiful memories with your new husband or wife.

## What Concerns Do You Have If One of You Has Children from a Previous Marriage?

When children come into a marriage from a prior marriage, it can raise the stress level of the marriage. If your future spouse has children who will be living with you, it's important to build trust and affection among you early on. It's also important to realize that as a stepparent you may never be able to replace the biological parent. The children will view you from an entirely different perspective. If you've had no previous experience with raising a child, it may be a difficult adjustment. Children don't disappear into the woodwork. They have many needs to be met, they make endless demands on your time, and their education and other expenses must be paid for.

Although the children may seem to support your relationship before the wedding, underneath they may be harboring mixed feelings. They may feel rejected when you move in, or they may fear losing other family relationships that are important to them. And possibly they may think their inheritance is at stake.

Holidays can become an issue between the divorced parents, and you'll have to decide which parent gets the children during holidays and summer vacation. You'll also have to think about what role you'll play in disciplining the children. Will they feel comfortable expressing their concerns and needs to you? What will they want and expect from you? These are all questions to explore with your future spouse and eventually the children.

 **Sid's Wisdom:** Talk over any commitments or promises your spouse may have made to his children. Solid communication on your part will help to make the children feel more secure in their new situation. Let your love for one another reach out and surround the children.

## *Do You Have Any Secrets You Want to Share?*

By the time you reach the stage in your life when you're discussing marriage, you already have a personal history. Chances are that there might be something in your past that you feel ashamed of and are afraid to talk about with your intended. You'll intentionally try to keep that part of yourself a secret. Perhaps you feel it's a secret so terrible that it would require a great deal of understanding and

51

acceptance from your partner—for example, a past criminal record, an abortion, a child you gave up for adoption, or the particulars of a messy divorce.

When you keep secrets from your loved one, it can adversely affect your entire relationship by creating barriers between you. You might not even be aware of it, but you may get defensive when a topic comes up that's suggestive of your secret. You may be unconsciously angry about the fact that you have this deep, dark secret locked away somewhere inside you. An extreme example of this would be if your intended never told you that he was previously married and had a child. Then one day a young man or woman shows up at your doorstep and says, "Hi, Dad!" Secrets like this can seriously affect a marriage.

If you trust the person you plan to marry, consider owning up to your past—the mistakes as well as the good experiences. Share your dreams and the things you feel might affect your relationship. One of the privileges of being married is to have someone you can trust with all your thoughts, hopes, and dreams. Hopefully, this process will end up being a strong bonding experience for the two of you.

**Sid's Wisdom:** Be careful about what secrets you decide to share. Disclosing secrets without thought to the consequences could do more harm than good. Make sure that what you share has some bearing on your marriage. Having children from a former marriage is relevant to your future marriage and should be talked about. Telling your fiancé every detail of a previous love affair is not necessary and will only hurt you both. Trust your mate-to-be to want to share your concerns and fears. Hopefully, this will lighten your load considerably.

*"Two monologues do not make a dialogue."*
**—Jeff Daly**

# Communication Skills

Communication is an important part of our life. It is, more than anything else, the essential element in maintaining a healthy relationship. How do you rate yourself in the area of communication skills? Think about it, because poor communication is one of the primary reasons for the breakup of a marriage.

Opening the doors to communication is not always easy. There are many personality types that don't communicate easily. These may include: the silent type (people who respond only when spoken to); people who are always on the defensive (if you say the sky is blue, they may argue with you); people who fear talking about the deeper questions in life; and those who can't tear themselves away from their work or the TV (they may prefer to avoid communicating altogether).

In addition, one of the biggest problems between couples is that they don't really listen. Typically, they interrupt each other or simply walk away. Poor communication is often the result of moving too quickly to solve the problem, without first trying to understand it.

Taking the time to listen and understand not only helps with better problem-solving but it first and foremost lets your partner know they're loved and important. Many problems that will come up in a marriage aren't there to be solved, but serve as an occasion to find out if indeed one is loved and important to their spouse. Just listening will solve the root issue of many problems.

Be a good listener. Be aware of your own thoughts and feelings and learn to express them clearly. Being defensive can quickly undermine the quality and content of your discussion, as can misdirected anger.

It's never too late to learn to communicate. It will take time to recognize and understand your differences, but being open and willing to listen and do so attentively is one of the first steps in the process of developing communication skills.

You will find some help in the many books that have been written in the past ten years about the differences between men and women that make communication difficult. As John Gray says in *Men Are from Mars, Women Are from Venus*, "Men and women differ in all areas of their lives. Not only do men and women communicate differently but they think, feel, perceive, react, respond, love, need, and appreciate differently. They almost seem to be from different planets, speaking different languages and needing different nourishment. . . . Understanding our differences helps resolve much of the frustration in dealing with and trying to understand the opposite sex. Misunderstandings can then be quickly dissipated or avoided. Incorrect expectations are easily corrected. When you remember that your partner is as different from you as someone from another planet, you can relax and cooperate with the differences instead of resisting or trying to change them."

# Are You Able to Express Your Innermost Thoughts?

You and your significant other have probably learned to communicate from your families. Therefore it follows that you most likely communicate differently, because one family's method of communication is different from the other's. For example, if you grew up in a household where your parents suppressed their feelings and kept their relationship on a superficial level, then that's what may occur in your own relationship.

Being able to express your innermost thoughts involves sharing your emotions and experiences with your loved one. Verbal intimacy requires a strong desire to know each other's deepest thoughts and concerns. It also requires that you know a lot about yourself. Many people go through life without getting to know themselves, which is, more often than not, a hindrance when trying to establish a meaningful relationship. It's one thing to have common interests and knowledge of each other's past; it's another to be able to reveal your total self to the other person, without fear of destroying the relationship, which is what intimacy is all about.

 **Sid's Wisdom:** If you can't talk to your potential spouse about what matters most to you, they may not be the right one for you and you should reconsider your future together.

# Are You Able to Communicate Your Love for One Another?

Everyone likes to hear words of love from their intended marriage partner. Unfortunately, even when two people genuinely love each other, they're often not adept at the language of love. How can you learn to express your love for one another? What little things can you do to say that you care?

Saying "I love you" is a warm and affectionate way to let your partner know how you feel. However, these words are only one means of communicating your love. A special compliment, a look from across the room, a kiss on the back of the neck, a hug in the kitchen during meal preparation, are all ways of saying "I love you." There are hundreds of unique expressions of love and affection. Some are verbal, like giving praise or offering to help with a particular problem; others are physical, like bestowing hugs or holding hands.

Even when doubt enters your mind and you think your mate doesn't love you anymore because he's not saying it or showing it, try to remember that love endures during these times. Don't hesitate to show your love or communicate your need for affection. Hopefully, he'll respond in kind.

**Sid's Wisdom:** If you're getting married to someone who you know truly loves you but has a hard time expressing it, then let him know what you want. Let it be known that you appreciate flowers or a romantic dinner. Sometimes that's all it takes to get the romance back on track.

# Do You Find It Easy to Talk to One Another about Your Daily Concerns?

There are probably times when you find it easier to talk to your mate than other times. Have you ever stopped to figure out why? Did it have to do with the surroundings you were in? When you both had more time available? When you were away from the daily grind? During times of crisis? Try to determine when the two of you are able to talk comfortably. If having a picnic in the park is conducive to good communication, plan more picnics. Times of crisis can be one of the important times for couples to talk openly.

Being easy to talk to means both of you taking a sincere interest in what the other person is saying and maintaining eye contact. Ask questions, make suggestions, and add comments that guide the conversation along smoothly. Being easy to talk to means you don't become defensive or talk down to your partner. Each should help create an atmosphere of cooperation, rather than conflict. The words you use, the tone of your voice, and your body language all have to do with the total message you send to your loved one.

**Sid's Wisdom:** Set aside time to share ideas, dreams, hopes, and fears with the most important person in your life. During conversations, let your partner know that you've heard what he had to say and, if necessary, ask if you've heard him correctly. This will help to avoid confusion and misunderstanding between the two of you.

# Are You an "I'm Right, You're Wrong" Kind of Person?

Would you rather be "right" or be willing to give in? There may be times when you think you're clearly right and your partner is dead set wrong. You'll feel angry, frustrated, and upset by the whole experience. No matter what you say, your spouse will not admit to being wrong. He just has to be right. As a result, your discussion turns into a fierce argument. He still won't give in, no matter how right you believe yourself to be. The outcome: communication meltdown! Again the question, Would you rather be right or be willing to negotiate a resolution?

If you get into the stubborn situation of "I'm right, you're wrong," different beliefs may be the problem. If you can't see each other's point of view, this may be one of those times when you must agree to disagree. If you don't value your mate's viewpoint, in essence you're saying, "I have nothing to learn from you; I'm always right, no matter what." Believe me, it's really okay to occasionally see things differently. If you regard every person whose way of thinking is different from yours as a threat, you're only doing yourself harm and you'll suffer the consequences.

 **Sid's Wisdom:** Seeing things differently doesn't mean that one person is right and the other wrong. It simply indicates a difference of opinion.

# Do You Take Each Other Seriously When Needed and Truly Listen?

When you live with someone on a daily basis, it's comfortable to be able to relax around each other, but there are times when a particular situation requires one or the other's undivided attention. Keep in mind that what may seem important to one of you may not seem so important to the other. However, a consistent lack of serious consideration may damage your relationship. It's important to know each other well and become aware of the need to listen to each other's concerns.

You become a good listener when you give your partner your full and undivided attention and eliminate any distractions in your immediate surroundings. This means getting away from the telephone and any other disruptions. Try to listen without judging or evaluating the circumstances from your point of view. Being a good listener means giving the other person what they want rather than what you think they should want.

Marriage can be an isolating situation when your loved one is the only one you can turn to for support in matters of money, children, and friendships. As you spend more and more years together, hopefully you become more in tune with your spouse and heed the times you need to listen to each other. It's important to be aware of the fact that your spouse will need the love and attention from someone he trusts. That trust allows him to feel safe and comfortable in sharing his deepest concerns and needs. Marriage can provide that trusted person, but if it doesn't, then there's something missing in your relationship. If you truly love someone, then your first consideration is for their welfare in all aspects of life.

**Sid's Wisdom:** Your spouse is your closest friend. Be open with each other and feel comfortable in sharing every aspect of your lives with one another. Become a good listener in your relationship with your partner. You can learn a lot about each other by lending an ear when it's most needed.

*"Personality is the name we give to our little collection of funny ways."*
—Source Unknown

# *Character Traits and Personality*

In a perfect world, what type of personality would you like your future mate to have? How would you prefer that she interacts with others? Do you want her to be very outgoing and aggressive, or laid back and easy-going? Would you like someone who is lighthearted or serious? Do you want someone who is sophisticated or down to earth and practical?

Of course, there's no perfect world, but it's a good idea to find a life partner whose personality is compatible with yours. Conflicting personality and character traits can become annoying over time. Since you'll be living with this person for a very long time, you don't want someone whose personality will irritate you day in and day out. No one is perfect, but you need to select someone with a personality you can appreciate and enjoy.

Most couples contemplating marriage approach it optimistically and don't think about the character traits that might become bothersome over time. However, it's an important consideration to keep in mind. Harmony exists in a relationship where the two intermingling personalities express their love for each other and don't allow the little things they may find annoying about the other person to bother them.

# Is Your Intended the Silent Type or a Babbling Brook?

There are some things you can't possibly know about your partner until you're married. Nevertheless, there are many characteristics you can pay attention to during the getting-to-know-one-another stage that will help you determine if he or she is right for you. One of them has to do with how communicative each of you is on an regular basis. If one of you always talks a lot and the other is generally very quiet, how will this affect your relationship over the long term?

Communication styles that are very different often pose a problem. Verbally articulate people like to converse. Reticent types usually prefer to listen or enjoy silence. Being opposite in this way can still work, providing you both have patience, are flexible, and respect each other's desire to communicate or not communicate.

Whatever the case may be, communication, in whatever form, is the name of the game in a successful marriage. The willingness to discuss things is important. Discussion allows for decision-making, and decision-making brings about desired results. No marriage will survive complete silence.

 **Sid's Wisdom:** Being flexible like bamboo instead of rigid like steel can save your marriage from the many differences that may become apparent after you're wed. Keep in mind that there are no two people who are totally alike in the entire world. Be prepared for, and enjoy, the differences in your communication styles.

# On a Scale of One to Ten, How Important Is a Sense of Humor to You?

When you ask your potential spouse this question, I hope he or she answers with at least an eight. A sense of humor can get you through some of the roughest times in a marriage. Of course, there are times when putting a humorous spin on things may not be appropriate. The key here is to find a happy medium.

Are you most attracted to serious-minded people or the happy-go-lucky kind? The melding of different kinds of personalities is not easy. A mate with a witty sense of humor can be the life of a party. If you don't share this talent or admire it, you might end up feeling left out of the fun. Or perhaps you have a dry sense of humor that your counterpart doesn't comprehend or appreciate.

The ability to laugh at yourselves and to find the same kinds of situations humorous are an important ingredient in handling stress in your relationship. Just keep in mind that there are many personalities in the world, and hopefully you'll end up with someone whose personality will make you smile through the years—and through the tears.

 **Sid's Wisdom:** Develop a lightheartedness within your relationship. Life is more enjoyable when you don't take every little thing that happens too seriously. It's amazing how a good laugh can clear the air.

# Is Making Up Easy or Hard to Do?

Is your partner the kind of person who holds resentment and has a hard time resolving differences? As a child, was he persistent in always getting his way? If so, are you prepared to live with this individual for a lifetime? How your significant other resolves differences is another area that may not be so obvious until you begin to share your life on a daily basis.

Marriage is intended to be a give-and-take relationship. If you both agree to this going in, it'll be a lot easier. Being able to forgive the small differences, and the larger ones as well, is a quality you'll cherish in your mate. Being able to forgive not only sets yourselves free, but it also invites trust into your relationship. Think about the times you've already found your loved one holding a grudge. Was it resolved in a way that satisfied both of you?

Being unable to forgive is like a wound that festers. It never gets better until you apply the salve that clears up the condition.

 **Sid's Wisdom:** Don't let grudges become a way of life in your relationship. Learn to resolve your differences and move on. Life is too short to spend an unreasonable amount of time defending your beliefs. Know when to call a truce and be willing to negotiate in order to work things out.

# Is Your Lover Prone to Jealousy?

Nothing undermines trust in a relationship like jealousy. Watch out for a jealous mate—you might be with someone who is so possessive that you will suffer in the end. This type of person may be extremely attentive and wonderful to the point of bestowing many gifts upon you and wanting to spend all their time with you or monopolizing your time. At first you may be awestruck, but later you may feel totally smothered. Heed these warning signs. It's usually an indication of deep insecurity on the part of a jealous person.

Does your potential marriage partner give you room to enjoy the company of other people, or does he go nuts when he sees you having a good time with someone other than himself—especially if it's someone of the opposite sex? If he's open about your having friendships with the opposite sex, do you think his attitude will change once you're married? A woman I know told me her fiancé made it crystal clear that she was not to form friendships with other men for fear it would one day lead to an affair. She's very outgoing and already had a number of male friends, so this idea made her totally uncomfortable. In the end, they were unable to resolve this and didn't marry. They say "love is blind"—don't let blindness lead you into a marriage that's doomed to failure.

**Sid's Wisdom:** If you think your potential spouse has a tendency toward jealousy, take this as a sign of their deep insecurity. Don't enter into marriage blinded by "love." Talk to your mate, as well as to friends and family who know this person well, to determine if this is a potential irresolvable problem.

# Are You Willing to Arbitrate Your Differences?

A successful marriage requires lots of give and take, yet the ability to find a middle ground is sometimes difficult. Learning to meet your partner halfway will permit smooth sailing in a lot of situations. From disagreements about what you should wear to a party to where your children will be attending school, the way you choose to handle disputes becomes important. When you and your partner disagree, the truth is that each of you is most likely right about some part of the argument.

Once you realize there's a difference of opinion regarding something you both feel is important, it's a good idea to listen to each other's concerns and suggestions. If you can do this, you avoid standoffs and you create an atmosphere of cooperation rather than confrontation. Listening to one another also encourages you to open up and express more of your thoughts and feelings about the predicament than you would if you were deadlocked in an argument that neither of you can win.

**Sid's Wisdom:** Whenever you get into the "I'm right, you're wrong" mode, expand your viewpoint by taking time to listen to your partner and ask relevant questions. Give each other a few minutes to express different sides of the issue without interruption. A solution you hadn't thought of before may miraculously appear.

# How Will You Manage Anger in Your Relationship?

Anger has been called "the misunderstood emotion." Many books have been written on the subject of anger alone. It's not surprising, considering the large number of people who don't know how to express their anger constructively and all the domestic violence in today's society. The sheer amount of domestic violence is an indication of anger gone wrong.

Anger, in itself, is just one of many emotions of our human heritage. When emotional intensity in a relationship is at its peak, many couples become involved in destructive behavior like trying to change the other person, blaming each other, or holding their anger in and giving each other the silent treatment. Some people are more skillful in dealing with their anger than others. Take the time to discuss this important topic with your partner.

Sometimes couples get angry at each other and say things they later regret. When you get angry, for whatever reason, at your significant other, it may be a good time to ask yourself: "What am I really angry about?" "Is my anger a response to being hurt?" "Can I find a better way of handling it?" "Is there a way of expressing my anger safely?" "Should I take a walk, use a punching bag, or write down my feelings on a piece of paper and let it out of my system?"

Getting in touch with your anger before you strike out or withdraw not only diffuses a potentially hazardous situation, but it also gives you insight into why you're angry and may show you more skillful ways of dealing with it in the future.

**Sid's Wisdom:** When you get angry about something in your relationship, remember the adage that "anger" can be just one letter short of "danger." Also, be aware that the absence of expressed anger can be dangerous too. How skillfully you take note of and utilize your anger has a lot to do with how successful you are in your relationships and other facets of life.

# Are You a Compassionate Person?

What constitutes a compassionate person? The dictionary defines it as one who "shows compassion deeply, shows sympathy for another, with an urge to help." Are you that kind of person? Do you recognize this trait in your significant other? On a scale of one to ten, where do you place yourself and your mate when it comes to being compassionate? Is there a wide gap? For example, is there a great difference in your attitudes toward those less fortunate than you? Is one of you kind and caring toward animals and the other exceedingly uncaring?

A compassionate mate comes in handy when you're struggling with issues that don't involve her (like problems at work) or when you're having an argument and judging her unfairly. Simple kindness brings better results than anger or cutting words. A compassionate mate is likely to accept you with all your imperfections, which is an important ingredient in the unconditional love that's needed to create a flourishing marriage.

 **Sid's Wisdom:** Always remember that you have little control over how much kindness and compassion is shown to you, but you do have the capacity to be kind and compassionate toward others.

# Do You Consider Yourself
# a Perfectionist?

Do you agonize over making a mistake and, when you do, find it hard to learn from your mistake and move on? Do you constantly focus on both your own faults and the faults of others? Do you expect more of yourself than you should? If so, you may be a perfectionist, and you may need to remind yourself that you have a right to make mistakes, to be imperfect and, in turn, be more compassionate toward yourself. If you don't make some changes, you can expect to have some serious problems in your new relationship.

If, on the other hand, you're a person who lives in fear of displeasing your partner by doing things the "wrong way," you're most likely involved with a perfectionist— someone who obsessively demands perfection. This kind of person is difficult to live with on a daily basis because they tend to be faultfinding and overly critical of you as well as themselves. They're also inclined to be controlling. They may have a hard time opening up, they become upset easily, and they don't like being told what to do. They always have the right answers. They constantly correct every little thing you say or do.

People who strive for perfection may avoid things they can't do well. They wake up at zero every morning and feel they must reach perfection every day. They tend to see things in black and white. This can be extremely stress-producing. Can you live with someone who is not going to budge, because a so-called perfectionist is most likely not going to change?

**Sid's Wisdom:** If you see traits of excessive impatience or intolerance in your spouse-to-be, you might have a hard time discussing issues presented in this book. This is all the more reason to get to know and understand each other better! If it's perfection she's looking for, let it be known that in your world it doesn't exist and it's perfectly okay to make mistakes and have imperfections, which is all part of being a caring and understanding person. But don't expect her to change. If you do, you might want to think twice about getting married.

# How Will You Behave with Members of the Opposite Sex?

Is your future spouse flirtatious by nature? Was this part of your original attraction to her? If so, will this kind of behavior with members of the opposite sex be acceptable to you after you're married? Maybe your significant other centered her attention on you when you first met, but after a while you noticed her interest in you waning. As a result, you're not feeling as secure in the relationship as you once did. There's a big difference between her just being open and friendly with other men and coming on strong in a sexual way.

Extramarital affairs are one of many reasons for divorce. What starts out as a partner who flirts and is a looker may very well end up as a partner who cheats. The lack of sexual integrity in a mate can take various forms, such as inappropriately touching other people, leering at the bodies of the opposite sex, and making frequent sexual comments to you and others. If you feel uncomfortable with this type of behavior, don't rationalize your feelings or make excuses for your partner. Get it out in the open and discuss your personal feelings. Ignoring it won't make it go away.

 **Sid's Wisdom:** Be careful that you don't mistake gregariousness for flirting. There's no problem with being friendly with the opposite sex, and if you really watch, you'll notice that a gregarious person is friendly with both sexes. Flirting, however, is another thing and should be taken seriously.

## *Are You Open to Counseling?*

Some clergy will not perform the marriage ceremony without a couple having at least several hours of premarital counseling, which is aimed at helping the couple learn more about the person they intend to marry. If premarital counseling is available to you, why not take advantage of it? You have nothing to lose and everything to gain.

Nevertheless, no matter how well you get to know your partner before marriage, there's always room for the unfortunate surprise. This may come in the form of some kind of unexpected behavior, resulting in what may appear to be an irreconcilable difference. If this should happen, counseling affords you the opportunity to meet with a qualified third party who can move discussions along hopefully to a favorable outcome and spare the possible need for a separation or divorce.

Too often, however, one person refuses to seek outside help. This leaves the other person feeling that her spouse is not living up to his half of the bargain—namely, to love, honor, and cherish through every kind of circumstance for as long as he lives. Many marriages break up because one or both in the partnership is not willing to work as hard as they might to make the relationship emotionally healthy. They usually blame the marriage for not working, when in fact they weren't willing to take the necessary steps to make it work. Unless major changes are made in their attitudes toward marriage, divorce will be a foregone conclusion.

**Sid's Wisdom:** Make a pact with your partner before you get married that both of you are willing to seek professional help in the event your marriage becomes so troubled that there seems to be no way to make it work.

*"A sense of values is the most important single element in human personality."*
—Source Unknown

# Personal Values and Ethics

It's important in a marriage to respect each other's values and ethics. This means getting to know each other on a deeper level than what you might accomplish after a few dinner dates. It requires finding out how much importance each of you places on spiritual life, integrity, fidelity, and family concerns, including the way money is spent, commitment to the community, etc. For example, would it be acceptable to you if your spouse borrowed money from a family member or friend and, without regret, never paid it back? How would you react?

Having different opinions and different ways of approaching things can be dynamite in a marriage (just make sure it's not too explosive). Be sure you can both laugh about your differences. When you love one another deeply, these differences won't affect your marriage to any great extent.

Your values and ethics are usually formed from the kind of upbringing and education you had. If your upbringing is comparable to your potential mate's, then your values will tend to be similar. Hopefully, things like different eating habits and health habits may not become major issues. Taking note of the way your intended treats others is also telling of his or her values.

Moral beliefs come into play when talking about values and ethics. Maybe your partner thinks you're silly for waiting to have sex. He wants you to jump into bed with him on your first date. You, on the other hand, want to experience some emotional intimacy first. Are your wishes respected? Perhaps you want the two of you to have an AIDS test before sleeping together. He jokes about the idea and refuses on the ground that it isn't really necessary and you should trust him. Watch out for that one!

Don't compromise your beliefs and interests. Find out about the values of your prospective partner at the beginning of your relationship. It may spare you some agonizing moments in the future.

# Are You Liberal-Minded or Conservative?

This is a question that's often overlooked when two people are contemplating marriage. When you go to the polls to vote, the decision as to which candidate or cause to support often lies in your attitude regarding liberal or conservative issues. Such attitudes can enter into a marriage relationship. Politically speaking, being a Democrat or a Republican may not be so different these days. Even your respective viewpoints about gun control and the death penalty may not make or break a marriage. However, it's wise to keep in mind that liberal and conservative attitudes can permeate a marriage on many levels. If you're a liberal-minded person and your mate is extremely conservative, you might end up being diametrically opposed regarding a lot of issues within the marriage such as what schools you send your children to, who your friends are, and what you do with your spare time. Political differences can make for interesting and lively discussions, but don't let politics destroy your love and respect for one another.

 **Sid's Wisdom:** Everything from one's relationship to money to style of dress is influenced by liberal or conservative thinking. Openly discuss your comfort level about these issues to determine any potentially serious trouble spots.

# Do You Have Strong Political Views?

Politics makes strange bedfellows, or so they say. What are your reactions to this claim? Are you and/or your potential spouse heavily involved in politics, or do you stand on the sidelines and put in your two cents' worth when you feel you have something to add? If either of you has a strong desire to get involved in political causes or run for office, these are the kinds of issues that need to be discussed prior to getting married. Perhaps one of you will want to make a major donation to a political cause or campaign that the other opposes. Would you be able to resolve this amicably? So often, topics that seem immaterial prior to marriage create friction and become major issues after marriage.

 **Sid's Wisdom:** As regards politics, the two of you may not agree on every issue, but when issues arise where there's a difference of opinion, respect each other's viewpoints. If necessary, agree to disagree on some things.

# Will Your Future Mate Be Willing to Volunteer Time in the Community or At Least Support You in Doing So?

The spirit of volunteerism exists in the minds and hearts of many people, both young and old. It's important when choosing a marriage partner that you be aware of their attitude toward helping others. If you have a desire to share your interests and talents with those who are less fortunate than yourself, most likely it'll require time away from home. Would your prospective partner agree to that?

You may have acquaintances who are in need of a helping hand, due to lack of child care, illness, or aging. Or you may simply enjoy becoming a part of a group that accomplishes things that will benefit the community. Would your newly beloved encourage you to ·do what you can, even though it means less time for each other or the family?

It's been pointed out that those who volunteer live longer and happier lives. Through volunteering you make new friends and you have opportunities to learn new talents. Volunteering as a couple can unite you in a different and more rewarding way than just sitting around the house watching TV or taking part in less rewarding activities.

 **Sid's Wisdom:** Sharing with your mate-to-be experiences where you felt needed and found rewards in helping others will help to bring into focus the type of persons both of you are. It can also make a difference in how you view each other.

# Is Honesty Your Best Policy?

What do you consider a lie? In other words, how honest are you about minor things? It's hard to imagine a person who hasn't at one time told a little white lie. For example, have you ever told your boss you were late for work because of a flat tire when in reality you overslept? Fibs like this aren't meant to hurt anyone. However, if a person gets into the habit of telling white lies, how will this affect their judgment about larger issues?

There are great benefits to not lying in a relationship. When you lie to your partner, you break a sacred bond of trust. Even if you think your partner may not like the truth, the rewards for telling the truth will come in time. Some people tell lies because telling the truth makes them feel less than perfect or they're unwilling to accept responsibility for doing something. There's no good reason for lying. If you're faced with a liar, be careful. Spending years with a liar can only end up with your guessing a lot about the relationship. Lying is a way of life for some people, but it's never a part of a happy and successful marriage.

**Sid's Wisdom:** If you suspect your mate-to-be is lying to you, bring the situation out in the open and ask for an explanation. If he admits to it, makes a suitable apology, agrees there will be truthful communication between the two of you, and it's something you can live with, forgive and move on.

# What Are Some of the Strengths Each of You Will Bring to the Marriage?

One of the things needed to adequately evaluate a partner-in-life is to get to know as much about him as you know about yourself. The better you get to know someone, the more you can appreciate and respect their strengths and become aware of their shortcomings and potential difficulties.

Each of you will no doubt bring different strengths and talents to your marriage, and these are marvelous gifts to be explored. Seek out and identify your individual talents. At the same time, learn to accept relatively insignificant shortcomings of yourself and your loved one. Both of you don't have to be perfectly skilled in all things. For example, maybe your partner has a knack for putting things together, but you can't hit a nail on its head to save your life. On the other hand, you're an accomplished cook, but your mate isn't able to tell an egg beater from a meat grinder. Be assured that if each of you is doing the best you're capable of doing, you'll complement each other and learn from one another throughout your years together.

**Sid's Wisdom:** Instead of always wishing that your partner was better at things, appreciate and welcome the strengths and talents he does have. Develop a balanced and lighthearted attitude about each other's shortcomings and there will be less tension in your marriage.

# Who Are Your Role Models?

Children often seek role models who represent the direction they wish to take in life. There's a lot to learn even as an adult from others who have been successful in relationships and other aspects of living.

It might be interesting for you and your mate to talk about your respective role models and couples you see as role models, because this could well give you some added insight into each other's desires and the type of person you're thinking of marrying. History abounds with wonderfully devoted couples. Robert Browning and Elizabeth Barrett Browning fell in love by reading each other's poetry, even before they met. Freud had a very special relationship with his wife, Anna. Paul McCartney and his wife, Linda, were happily married until her premature death from cancer in 1998. It doesn't matter if your future mate's role model is a famous sports figure, a well-known person in history, a parent, or a special neighbor who has given guidance. The idea is to learn whatever you can about this role model in order to better understand and appreciate the aspirations of your beloved.

**Sid's Wisdom:** Many times, as you inquire about each other's role models, you'll find that both of you have some of the same expectations and dreams for the future. This provides you with the opportunity to develop your lifestyle around such models.

*"A marriage may be made in heaven, but the maintenance must be done on Earth."*

—**Source Unknown**

# Professional Life, Work, and Career

For some people, the job they do pretty much defines who they are because they make work a priority in their lives. Others work to be able to live a full life rather than live just to work. They strive for more balance between work and enjoyment.

The questions in this section are being posed so that you can sort out your feelings about work-related issues and how these issues will be adapted to your living together and future family responsibilities. Generally, in today's world, both partners in a marriage work so they'll have a comfortable lifestyle. This means that roles within the household need to be more clearly defined, and the time you spend together will have to be negotiated to the satisfaction of both of you. If your spouse puts in significant overtime at the office or is expected to wine and dine clients every night, when does that leave time for the two of you, or eventually your family?

Couples who take the time to visualize their future

together prior to marriage can avoid some heated debates after marriage as to who is going to sacrifice what to whom when it comes to their careers and future lifestyle. Don't assume it'll just work itself out.

# Do You Appreciate and Value Your Future Spouse's Career?

It's important that both partners in a relationship support what the other does for a living and take a sincere interest in that work. For example, if your future mate's line of work is totally foreign to you, you may have to ask a lot of questions about it. For many couples, the dinner table is a place where work is a topic of discussion. If you sit there with a bored or vacant look on your face because you don't relate to the commodities market or a particular client problem, don't blame your spouse-to-be for feeling rejected because you're not interested. Take an active interest in learning about each other's careers, because it'll be an integral part of your future together. The kinds of careers you choose will influence your daily life—from the amount of time you spend together and the way you spend it, to the kind of lifestyle you can comfortably afford.

If your partner doesn't enjoy his or her line of work, perhaps you'll need to support a career change or encourage enrollment in a continuing education program, or whatever is most appropriate. It's well known that most people in this day and age change careers many times. Work together to try to find happiness, as well as success, in your fields of endeavor.

 **Sid's Wisdom:** Encourage each other to seek happiness in the work you do. Support your partner if she wants to make a change, even though it might not be as financially rewarding in the short run.

# Do Your Working Hours Coincide?

A majority of people spend most of their twenty-four hours sleeping and working. Six to eight hours of sleep is normal. However, some people work many more hours than others, either because their jobs demand it or they're workaholics. This may not leave much time to spend together. That's why it's important to discuss your respective working hours and arrange quality time to be together. This might end up being dinnertime or taking a walk together in the mornings before heading off to work.

Days off and vacations are also things to think about. If one of you works at home on your own time or is a freelancer, and the other must keep strict hours at the office and possibly put in overtime, how will you deal with planning weekends and taking vacations? Moments of unexpected or planned happiness are hard to come by when work schedules don't coincide.

Spending as much time together as possible is important for a good marriage. If you find yourselves spending a lot of time apart, then you should make adjustments. For example, would you be willing to look for a job that allowed you to spend more time together? Could you plan a "date night" each week and do something unusual, exciting, or romantic? When a marriage becomes so routine that it has no surprises, no special moments, then you need to sit down and put aside at least an hour or two a week when you can enjoy each other's company.

 **Sid's Wisdom:** Make sure that the person you intend to marry agrees with you that spending time together is important.

# Do You Foresee Plans for Continuing Education?

Do your future plans in life include going back to school to get a degree? Will your chosen work require additional classroom training at some point? When young couples marry, it's understandable that one or both may not yet have attained the level of education they desire.

The rewards of education are many. Formal education can be undertaken for the simple pleasure of learning new things or for preparing oneself for a job or career in a chosen field. Attaining educational goals often requires one of you to sacrifice your own goals for a period of time so the other can reach his or her objective. How would you feel about having to set aside your dreams for a while so that your spouse can go back to the classroom? What effect would this have on your marriage? It's important to discuss the pros and cons of such a decision well before you take your marriage vows.

 **Sid's Wisdom:** Share all your aspirations with your potential spouse and plan your dreams together at the start of your relationship. This will help to put you on the road to a successful and satisfying marriage.

# Are Your Ambition Levels Somewhat Equal?

Couples who have a similar amount of inner drive for what they want in life will have a more balanced relationship throughout their years together. Take a reading of your potential mate's level of ambition. Does he consider work just a way of making money and paying the bills, or does he have a burning desire to attain prominence in his field? Is he content to put in his forty hours a week at his job and spend the rest of his time enjoying other activities such as playing tennis or watching sports on television? Are you much more ambitious than your future mate? Does your future spouse have the same commitment to his career as you do to yours? Is your ambition to work at home?

The issue of ambition levels can become a stickler in a marriage, especially when you have goals that aren't being met such as buying a house or a new car, taking regular vacations, and hundreds of other things. Many marriages fail because one person persists in living a free and easy lifestyle while the other works hard to achieve the family's goals. When you discuss professional goals and future objectives with your significant other, be sure there's an understanding on both sides to accept and support the other person in the lifestyle you both hope to achieve.

**Sid's Wisdom:** Give a lot of thought to each other's level of ambition. If they're significantly different, don't expect to be able to change your future partner's attitude toward this potentially volatile issue. Love does not always conquer all.

*"A good marriage is like a casserole: only those responsible for it really know what goes into it."*

**—Source Unknown**

# *Love, Sex, and Commitment*

When a relationship is new, sex often plays a big part in the time a couple spends together. The passion is new and the pleasure of discovering one another, gazing into each other's eyes, and feeling a special closeness appears to increase every day. Eventually, though, reality dawns and sex may taper off. Unless a couple has explored other aspects of their relationship, they may begin to feel like strangers to one another. If you think this may happen to you, take the opportunity to get to know and enjoy one another in other ways. Good sex is not the only ingredient in a gratifying marriage (albeit it's an important one).

Whether you have sex before marriage or wait until after you're married, it's important to understand each other's feelings about your future sexual relationship. The amount and frequency of sex is something that many couples disagree on. In a marriage relationship, it's important to feel loved without the priority being placed on sex. There are other ways of showing love, being intimate, and getting your emotional needs met. But if your partner loses interest in sex, it may indicate a problem with your relationship that needs to be talked about.

There may be times in your marriage when you feel unloved by your partner. Hurt, resentment, and criticism are all part of the struggles of married life. Just because the going gets rough doesn't mean you should divorce your partner. This is not a take-it-or-leave-it job. If you said the traditional vows in your wedding ceremony, you made a commitment "to have and to hold"—forever. Look for ways to solve your problems that bring pleasure and lightheartedness to the situation rather than gloom and doom. There are often lessons to be learned about yourself in the process that lead to an even stronger bond of love between the two of you.

# What Is the Meaning of Love for You?

Do you feel you understand what love is? Are you prepared to love your partner to the extent that you accept her for who she is and won't try to change her? Acceptance is a big part of love. If you think back to when you first said "I love you," chances are you were more accepting of her shortcomings then, or perhaps you weren't even aware of them. As you begin to discover each other's imperfections, it's possible that some conflict will enter the relationship. Each faultfinding thought and resentment you have toward your beloved affects your feelings of love for her. Try letting go of the desire to change your future spouse, and happiness may increase in your relationship.

You can't "win" love and affection from your significant other, nor should you try. Love, expressed naturally, doesn't take a lot of effort. The true expression of love becomes apparent through caring, kind words, or a gentle smile. Genuine love for one another should precede any selfish motive or expectation of love that you may hold in your hearts. Love is not something to be used in a controlling way. Neither is love an all or nothing deal. Take time to discuss with each other your perceptions of what love really means.

 **Sid's Wisdom:** Make loving choices for yourself and your loved one and the true nature of love will appear.

# What Does the Term "Enduring Love" Mean to You?

Many people believe that love is expressed purely in the physical sense. For others, the true expression of love becomes apparent through gestures and words that are part of their daily lives. What does "enduring love" mean to you? Is it the passionate, romantic love, that flying high feeling you experience when you're with your beloved? What happens when that fades and you need to move on to developing a deeper, more mature kind of love?

Enduring love can be a very involved process. To have enduring love, most couples go through several stages in their relationship. The romantic stage is the first and usually the most exciting. But don't fool yourselves into thinking that this alone constitutes enduring love.

Enduring love is many things. It means taking care of each other in sickness and in health, being there in times of joy and unhappiness, trusting each other, accepting one another as you are without wanting to change each other, and enjoying many interests in common. All these things contribute to a permanent love relationship. Take the time to discover each other's interpretation of enduring love. Be realistic about the effort that's needed to make your marriage successful.

 **Sid's Wisdom:** Take time to develop the skills that will lead to enduring love. Listen carefully to each other, respond openly and honestly, and pay attention to what's going on inside the other person. You may be surprised by what you find.

# Are You Getting Married for Reasons Other Than Love?

Marriages sometimes happen for matters of convenience or necessity. Individuals may desire companionship and marry for that reason. If a man or woman has children from a previous marriage, he or she may feel the need for the children to have both a mother and a father, and that becomes the priority rather than whether or not they're in love. An unmarried girl becomes pregnant, and the couple, in their desire to do the right thing, agree to marry. Then there are those who marry for money and security. I'm sure there are a lot of other reasons one could explore, and while nothing can guarantee a successful marriage, an ardent love has been known to develop in time between couples who marry for reasons other than love.

If you know you're marrying for reasons other than love, does your future spouse know it, too? If you're in agreement on your reasons for getting married, which do not include being in love, are you harboring any unrealistic expectations about the future of your marriage? For example, is one of you hoping that you'll be able to change your marriage of convenience into an impassioned one? Are you prepared for the fact that this might not happen but you'll still find happiness and commitment to the marriage?

 **Sid's Wisdom:** If you're getting married for reasons other than love, it may seem like an acceptable arrangement, but sincere and passionate love is an important ingredient in the successful union of two people planning to spend the rest of their lives together.

# Are You Physically Attracted to Your Intended Spouse?

Is there a strong sexual chemistry in your relationship or simply an admiration and liking for each other? If you haven't felt sexually attracted to your potential spouse from the start of your relationship, do you think it's possible to develop those feelings over time? Do you think it's feasible to have a healthy, lasting marriage with someone you're not physically attracted to?

Physical attraction between two people is an important ingredient if they're to sustain a fulfilling relationship. Important as it is, however, it's just ONE part of choosing the right partner. Too often the physical involvement is the overriding reason for getting married, when in fact there's so much more to marriage than simply enjoying the sexual aspects of it.

In the beginning of your relationship, passionate lovemaking has a way of blinding you to other important emotional and spiritual considerations. What happens when the feelings of intense passion fade? Will you be able to make the passage from a wild passionate love to a deeper, more mature kind of love? This is where a lot of couples get stuck. They don't develop what's needed along the way to get them to the next level in their relationship—such as good communication, caring, affection, and support for one another.

 **Sid's Wisdom:** Make sure that the right kind of chemistry exists between the two of you before you get seriously involved in considering marriage.

# Are You on the Same Wavelength When It Comes to Meeting Your Partner's Sexual Needs?

One of the biggest potential trouble spots in a marriage is the issue of sex. If your spouse loses interest in sex for weeks at a time, how will you deal with it? Generally speaking, when sex isn't great for one or both of you, a tremendous amount of focus is put on its absence, and conflicts can arise. On the other hand, when sex in the marriage is going great, it rarely gets mentioned. The level of a couple's sexual satisfaction often reflects what's going on in their relationship. If there's a lot of discord or if their friendship has cooled, then there probably isn't much excitement in the bedroom.

What you give to each other in your relationship should not be based on expectations of sex. Sex is not a condition of love, but a choice. If there are times when you feel pressured by your partner, try to express your feelings in a gentle and loving way. If you're the one who wants sex and your spouse doesn't, try to respect his or her wishes.

 **Sid's Wisdom:** In order to develop a healthy sexual relationship with your partner over the long term, you need to have a solid base of intimacy, compatibility, and commitment to one another.

# Is Romance Important?

"Romance" is a magic word. It conjures up the image of an exotic island in the South Seas with natives in colorful dress, music lilting in the background, and lovers eating coconuts all day long. For others, it may be having the man of your dreams take you in his arms under a star-filled sky and tell you he loves you. If either of these is your idea of romance, how will you continue to include it in your marriage?

Most couples have dreams of keeping the passion in their marriage forever. Have you ever wondered how you'll achieve this dream in your daily routine of getting up in the morning, seeing the kids off to school, going to work, and then coming home tired? Romance begins in the heart, and one of the greatest pleasures in marriage is feeling that your spouse genuinely loves you and cares about you. This means coming home at the end of the day, putting your arms around each other, asking each other how your day was, and really listening and sharing. And don't forget a kiss or two. Too often, after years of living together, the relationship goes on automatic pilot. It's at this point that the possibility of romance gets lost. Don't let it!

 **Sid's Wisdom:** Romantic interludes are much more meaningful when you and your mate relate to each other in loving and caring ways on a day-to-day basis.

# How Much Sexual Experience Have You Had?

If you've had a lot of experience with sex and your partner hasn't, or vice versa, how will this affect the first time you have sex together? Has one or the other of you had a bad sexual experience in the past? It's especially important to discuss any sexual doubts or insecurities with your mate prior to engaging in intimate relations. There are both physical and mental aspects to lovemaking, and the two of you will want to feel at ease with each other in the bedroom.

Sharing your sexual experience with your significant other shouldn't require delving into every detail of his or her prior sexual relations. However, each person brings to the relationship certain expectations about sex and sexual roles. This includes how often you want to have sex, who should make the first move, if you like to talk during lovemaking, and what kinds of things turn you on or off during sex.

If one of you is a virgin, extra care and patience should be shown. It's often assumed that good sex will come naturally and easily to two people who love each other. Even in the case of experienced couples, there may be a period of getting used to each other's wants and likes. Be patient with each other. You'll have plenty of time to learn to enjoy each other physically.

 **Sid's Wisdom:** Cultivating a healthy sexual relationship with your spouse takes time, thoughtfulness, and a respect for each other's values.

# Do You Have Hang-Ups with Sex?

Each partner in a marriage has a natural expectation of giving and receiving loving physical intimacy. An aversion to sex can come from many places, such as a fear of intimacy, rape, or childhood sexual molestation. It can even stem from being told as a child that sex is dirty.

What happens if you've remained celibate prior to marriage and afterward discover that your mate has a serious hang-up with sex? Don't avoid dealing with the matter. Seek professional help immediately. It'll save you a lot of frustration and heartache. This kind of problem results in feelings of rejection, hurt, anger, and confusion. Sexual dysfunction often requires professional help. You owe it to your partner and yourself to seek help so that you can enjoy a healthy sex life together.

**Sid's Wisdom:** If you encounter serious sexual problems in your relationship, keep the lines of communication open with your partner, seek professional counseling, and take comfort in the fact that many times it's a medical problem and can be corrected.

# Do You Have Any Bizarre Sexual Addiction or Habits?

This may seem like a strange question to ask the one you plan to marry, but how would you react if after you're married you discover that your partner loves phone sex or wants to watch pornographic videos with you or without you? There are all kinds of sexual obsessions out there, yet it's unlikely you would detect this type of behavior easily, especially at first. Nor is it probable your mate would openly reveal such conduct to you. If he's scared he has a fetish you'd consider perverted, he'd probably feel safer keeping it to himself for as long as possible.

It's important to discuss what each of you is comfortable with sexually and what you would find unacceptable. Talking about such issues and listening to each other's thinking before you commit to marriage gives you both a chance to explore your beliefs and values in this highly sensitive area. If you do discover something bizarre that you wouldn't allow in your sexual relationship, ask your partner to seek professional help. If he seems willing to work on the problem, then perhaps you can work it out.

**Sid's Wisdom:** Part of being intimate is being comfortable in sharing your most private and personal thoughts with the one you love. Sexual addictions and obsessions can destroy intimacy because they may humiliate or dominate the sexually healthy person in the relationship.

# Were You Friends Before You Were Lovers?

You probably have had at least one best friend in your life, someone you telephoned in the middle of the night with your troubles, someone you knew would be there because she's always been a support to you. Your spouse-to-be should also be your best friend—a confidant. A great marriage partner encourages, motivates, and listens to you—even challenges you at times. He helps you sort through your thoughts and feelings and confront your problems. When you have this kind of friendship along with an exciting love partner, you're headed in the right direction for a lifetime of happiness.

When you see yourself as a lover first and a friend second, it may be time for you to take notice of the direction your relationship is heading. In marriage, when couples lose their feeling of being friends, that's when a marriage can fall apart. Think about it this way: Would you treat a best friend without respect? Would you make un-called-for demands upon her time? Would you refuse to spend quality time with that person? If you don't see your future spouse as your best friend, it's time to make a sincere effort to establish that relationship before marriage. Express your love for one another in all that you say and do.

 **Sid's Wisdom:** When there is true friendship involved in a marriage, the results can be beyond your expectations.

# Will You Accept Each Other As You Are?

Some of the worst moments in a marriage happen when one person tries to change something about the other. This may take time, because when your relationship is new, your partner's imperfections may not seem significant to you. When you marry and it becomes a twenty-four-hour-a-day, seven-day-a-week relationship, will you be ready to put up with some of those irritating things that you overlooked earlier on?

If you find yourself aggravated by something your mate does, step back and take a look at yourself. It could be that something you do brings about the unwanted response, such as the way you handle a problem or react to a criticism. But if you truly feel the need to suggest that your partner change in some major way, get it out in the open before you get married. If it doesn't change before the wedding, it's a good possibility it won't change afterwards.

 **Sid's Wisdom:** Unconditional love asks that you let go of trying to change your spouse. Acceptance is a big part of a good relationship. It's likely that when you let go of your desire to change your partner, you'll gain peace of mind, and more satisfaction in your relationship may be the result.

# Do You View Marriage as Something Worth Trying, but if It Doesn't Work Out, You Can Try It Again with Someone Else?

Marriage is meant to be a lifetime commitment to another human being. What guidelines have the two of you created that help guarantee a lifetime of love and devotion to one another? What does commitment really look like? When you say your wedding vows, whether you write them yourself or use the traditional language, you make some pretty awesome promises that you intend to keep forever, not only when it's convenient and easy.

Unfortunately, in today's world, being in a committed relationship doesn't carry the weight it once did. For some people, commitment is passé. A truly committed relationship is considered somewhat archaic. Society now accepts a couple who will walk out of a marriage if the going gets too tough. It's true, though, that sometimes marriage is so difficult that keeping your promise seems impossible. That's exactly when a committed partner can make all the difference. If you know deep down that your spouse is committed to your lifelong relationship, then there's a feeling of security and less fear of abandonment in troubled times. If, in turn, you're married to someone who thinks they can trade you in like an unwanted piece of furniture, what kind of marital security do you have?

**Sid's Wisdom:** Until you believe you can honestly make a lifelong commitment to your potential partner, you shouldn't even consider taking the marriage vows. Without an honest commitment, there's little room for trust or intimacy between two people.

## What Is Your Level of Commitment—in Sickness and in Health?

"For richer or for poorer, for better or for worse, in sickness and in health . . ." Of all the words in the traditional wedding vows, these may be the least heard. This is not so strange, in light of the fact that couples who marry are looking forward to building a life together; they're not thinking about sickness, death, and dying.

Nonetheless, marrying inherently means you intend to grow old together. No one is immortal in this life. Death is inevitable. If you truly commit yourself to the person you're about to marry, then the commitment shouldn't end if one of you becomes severely disabled or ill. On the other hand, if you've never been tested under such circumstances, it's hard to predict how you'll react. A life-threatening illness tests a marriage like nothing else. It can cause emotional havoc and financial stress in a family. I've watched couples who, when faced with serious illness, weather the storm and actually grow closer; other marriages deteriorate when challenged in this manner.

Remember, when you commit yourself to marriage, you need to ask each other if you're committing yourselves to love, honor, and cherish your mate until one of you dies. There's no question that all lifetime marriages go through times of distress. If your loved one becomes afflicted with a serious illness or disease, it's natural to experience feelings of grief, frustration, and even anger. This doesn't mean you stop loving the person. You continue to "love, honor and cherish for as long as you both shall live."

**Sid's Wisdom:** If you or your loved one is faced with ill health over the course of your relationship, go easy on yourself. You're only human and there will be limitations on what you can do. The important thing is to let your spouse know you love her—and to continue to show it in everything you say or do.

## How Would You React to Your Spouse Having an Affair?

This is a difficult question to discuss prior to marriage, but it should be considered. How would you respond if your husband or wife suspected you of cheating and hired a private detective to follow your every move? Or that if your spouse found out you were unfaithful, he or she would leave you in a split second? In reality, you may not know what your reaction would be, and hopefully, it won't become an issue.

Surveys have indicated that with nearly half of all married couples, one or the other will be unfaithful to their partner at some point during their lifetime together. However, according to marriage guru and psychology professor Dr. John Gottman, "Only twenty percent of divorces are caused by an affair." To my thinking, this means there must be a lot of forgiving going on. Gottman also asserts that "most marriages die with a whimper, as people turn away from one another, slowly growing apart."

Indeed, an affair can be a rude awakening for the cheated-on spouse. It can also be looked upon as a valuable wake-up call for the couple. No matter what problems you may have in your marriage, having an affair will only add to them. How will you rebuild trust in the relationship? How will you deal with the serious hurt, feelings of betrayal, and anger that such an event causes? Would you both be willing to take a closer look at your marriage to see what's not working and work on rebuilding it in a loving and forgiving way to make it better than ever? Or would you just walk away and file for divorce? Would your response be different if there were children involved? The knowledge you gain from your significant other regarding this question might make you think twice about saying "yes" to marrying him.

 **Sid's Wisdom:** If you become unhappy in your marriage, don't look to someone outside it for love and understanding. Determine what went wrong. Realize that there's something that needs to be fixed and make an effort to work together with your spouse to rebuild your relationship to the satisfaction of both of you.

# Money and Finances

Unfortunately, two people can't live on love alone. As much as we wish it weren't so, in our world money is important. Many marriage break-ups, possibly most, are because of finances. If money doesn't actually cause a divorce, arguing over money can often become the most destructive element in a marriage.

Regardless of your age, money and finances require your immediate attention. Young people especially may have little or no experience in handling money. They've either just gotten out of high school and have their first, low-paying job, or they've just graduated from college, having spent a huge chunk of other people's money— usually Mom and Dad's hard-earned dollars. Marriage frequently is the joining together of two inexperienced financial wizards who are used to having their parents provide housing, food, and pocket money.

Financial hardship in a marriage can affect the couple's relationship in a number of ways. It can put unwanted stress on them by having to juggle bills constantly and worry about how to make ends meet. Perhaps one or both of them will have to take on a second job to pay the bills, resulting in less time spent with each other.

The questions in this section are meant to help you discuss your individual attitudes toward money going into the marriage, how you'll handle finances within the relationship, and what your financial goals for the future might look like.

# Who Will Be the Primary Earner?

Generally speaking, in today's society, both partners in a marriage go out and earn their combined income to make ends meet. One may bring home more money than the other or they may bring home equal paychecks. However, there's a trend to have one or the other at home when children enter the picture. It's even becoming more common for the wife to go out and work while the husband stays home and takes care of the children and domestic chores. This is often the case when the wife's salary far exceeds that of her husband's or when the husband's job becomes intolerable. Many couples live happily with this arrangement.

If you're planning to get married and haven't yet discussed the possibility of this happening after you take your vows, then this could be the one question in this book you need to discuss in depth. Don't get plagued by financial matters! If you're both earning a living when you get married and one of you becomes dissatisfied with your job, or you decide to have a child and want to be at home permanently, will the other person be able to take up the financial slack and become the primary earner? How will each partner handle this situation psychologically? This is surely food for thought.

 **Sid's Wisdom:** Let your thoughts be known as to to who should provide the primary financial support in the family.

# What Are Your Spending Habits?

There's nothing more frustrating for married people than a huge difference in the way money is spent. You probably already know if your significant other is a big spender or a penny pincher, but have you discussed how to resolve these issues once you're living under the same roof?

You may know that your future spouse is a clotheshorse or a shoe addict—you've seen her in action many times while you've been dating—and it hasn't concerned you so far. In contrast, you're satisfied with one new suit a year and once in a while a new pair of shoes. How will it affect you, after you're married, when she comes prancing through the door of your new heavily mortgaged home with more shopping bags than you can count, acting like Imelda II?

Perhaps you've been showering your fiancée with gifts and weekly bouquets of flowers during your courtship. Will you continue to do so after you're wed? Will she continue to expect such royal treatment and will you comply with the same desire to please? And what about all those expensive restaurant dinners you've wooed her with? Will she be willing to give those up in the interest of investing in your future together?

What you experience as a couple during the dating period may not be feasible when you have household expenses as well as the costs of raising a family.

 **Sid's Wisdom:** Don't let money, or the things that money can buy, become a disrupting issue between you.

# Do You Have Any Huge Outstanding Loans or Debts?

Can you imagine what it would be like to get married and then find out your spouse owes enormous amounts of money to family, friends, banks, and possibly even loan sharks? A good, workable marriage requires honesty with one another. Money matters need to be laid out on the table for open discussion prior to marriage. There should be some explanation of what financial debts each of you has and how you're going to settle them. It may be necessary to prepare a budget that you both agree on for the present as well as for the future. Living constantly above your means only adds to an already bad debt situation.

Money is an issue that hits people in their deepest pockets. For many people, so much of themselves is wrapped up in how much they have, how much they owe, and what more they want. Investigate thoroughly each other's money history. If neither of you has sufficient experience in financial matters, hire an adviser or seek advice from a family member or trusted friend.

 **Sid's Wisdom:** Entering into a marriage heavily in debt can cause worry and stress. Make sure spending habits are brought under control and debts paid off in a timely manner so that you can enjoy a harmonious future.

# What Is Your Attitude About Credit Cards?

When you think of credit card spending, what do you see? Do you visualize paying the balance off each month or making only the minimum payment? What credit cards are reasonable for each of you to use? Are you aware that the monthly interest credit card companies charge to their customers is what makes the companies rich—and you poor?

There's no doubt that credit cards are convenient and handy in many situations—when on a vacation, for example. For one thing, they provide you with a record of your purchases. For another, you don't have to carry cash for many of your purchases. On the other hand, credit cards often give you the feeling that you can afford to buy anything you want now and pay for it later.

When I think of credit card spending, I'm reminded of the story about a newly married couple who emigrated to the United States. Soon after their arrival, they were issued a credit card. They were excited and proceeded to furnish their entire house using the card. A few months down the line, when they weren't able to make the minimum payment, they were shocked and humiliated when the retail store showed up and repossessed everything they had purchased. An extreme but not uncommon example, this proves how lethal credit card spending can be if you don't plan your finances well.

**Sid's Wisdom:** If possible, pay off the balance each month. Being mired in credit card debt is a surefire cause of difficulty in a marriage. If you see that your finances are getting out of hand, get in touch immediately with one of the many organizations that specialize in consolidating your bills and paying them on time, at no extra cost to you. It's worth it not to ruin your credit record.

## Will You Have Separate Bank Accounts, a Joint One, or Both?

Marriage is all about sharing—sharing a home, food, perhaps a car, and household duties. When you have children, you share the responsibility of raising them. What about a shared bank account? Many couples, especially older ones, draw the line here for a number of reasons. One person may only balance his or her checking account monthly, while the other is meticulous about making entries on a day-to-day basis. They differ greatly when it comes to spending and saving habits. If one or both were married before and have children who still require financial support, then separate accounts make good sense. Then there's the issue of approval. Having separate accounts allows more freedom of spending so the couple doesn't have to run to each other for permission to buy something.

Don't let money come between you and a happy marriage. Make every effort to sit down beforehand to discuss what feels comfortable to both of you regarding the family ledger. Several options are available. Maybe you want to have a joint account for your usual monthly expenditures but separate accounts for the extras. I know couples who still open a Christmas Club account and independently contribute to it each month. Be creative! How about the old-fashioned change-in-the-jar-at-the-end-of-the-day routine as a special joint savings account to underwrite an occasional romantic weekend away from the everyday world?

**Sid's Wisdom:** In this instance, sharing relates to your future. Saving and spending your money together as partners may give you an added sense of togetherness and a heightened sense of trust in one another, not only in financial matters, but in all areas of your relationship.

# Who Will Be Responsible for Keeping Financial Records and Paying Bills?

It's important that one partner in a marriage be responsible for handling the finances. The final choice should be whoever has the most experience and is most concerned with the dollars spent. Often one partner lacks skill in this regard and finds that at the end of the month there's not enough money left in the bank account to cover all the bills.

Good financial planning includes not only what you need to consider regarding day-to-day finances, but also your future financial needs. In some marriages, one partner may come from a family that made it a practice to pay all the bills at the end of the month. In addition, they may have set aside enough money so that when vacation time rolled around, money was available for that purpose. Should sickness occur, there was money to cover such unexpected costs, or a good insurance plan was purchased in anticipation of such expenses. The list goes on and on as to what financial conditions might arise. Wouldn't it be nice if there was a little extra money available to buy some of the things that each of you would like? Talk your financial concerns over in advance of the wedding date and make sure both of you are in agreement as to who will handle your finances, and how.

 **Sid's Wisdom:** Financial security within a marriage is not based upon how much money you have, but how you handle the money you do have.

# How Will You Handle Your Major Assets Once You're Married?

If you're young and contemplating marriage, chances are you don't have a lot of property and large assets to bring into the picture. But if you do have a considerable amount of valuable property and belongings, what plans do you have for them? Would you consider selling your condo to buy a new house with your future spouse? Or can you afford to rent it out to provide some income for the future? What if one of you is about to inherit a fortune from a great-uncle? Will "what's mine is yours" hold true? Maybe you have two expensive cars between you or you've both made a number of investments in money market funds. What do you do? You need to decide what property to join together as joint common property of the marriage BEFORE you get wedded. You should make a list of what's joint property and what's to be separate property.

If your future spouse's priorities don't match yours regarding your various assets (what's his and what's yours), you could end up feeling resentful toward each other. Take time to discuss how you'll share—or not share. You may even want to draw up a prenuptial agreement to reduce any chances of misunderstanding. If so, each of you should be represented by your own lawyer who can advise you about your rights and obligations. In fact, some states require independent attorneys for the contract to be enforceable. Such planning put into writing will save much unhappiness and discord throughout your marriage.

 **Sid's Wisdom:** You may not think that money has any place in love, but it does, and you're better off planning for it.

# How Do You Foresee Planning for Retirement?

Financial planners will tell you that it's never too early to begin planning for retirement. It may not be your main concern as you enter into matrimony, especially if you're young and still preoccupied with education or looking to land your first big job. Soon, however, it will become important. Experts recommend that early in your marriage you should set aside a portion of your income, approximately ten percent, toward retirement. With the future of Social Security benefits uncertain, you may indeed need to create your own retirement plan, and many young people are doing just that.

Get to know one another well enough so that you can discuss future financial matters and feel comfortable with whatever planning you undertake. Some couples plan for an early retirement. If this is your intent, unless you're independently wealthy, you'll need to start saving or investing as early as possible. In all this planning, don't forget the fun part—dreaming about what kind of lifestyle you hope to have in your golden years and where you'd like to retire. Perhaps you have hopes for a second home in the Bahamas or you see yourselves globetrotting in your later years. Whatever your choices, you'll need to stash away some of that green stuff regularly, starting immediately!

 **Sid's Wisdom:** Dreaming together helps you set goals, and reaching your goals is part and parcel of a happy and successful marriage.

# How Would You Handle a Severe Financial Crisis?

If sex is one area of life that presents trouble in a marriage, money is the other. There's no doubt that the effects of money on a relationship can be wearisome if you don't have a financial plan. Even if you do have a good plan, a severe money crisis has the potential to wreak havoc on your marriage. During times of financial stress, tensions mount and some couples become obsessed with their problems. Others get into the blame game. The smart ones pull together and talk things through. They may even try to keep a sense of humor despite the potential for disaster.

In the past, when you experienced a financial problem, what did you do? Did you seek advice and concentrate on making the best of the situation, or did you react emotionally and hit the panic button. Often, a severe financial crisis is a wake-up call to other problem areas in your relationship. Your attitude toward money can divide a family rather than make it stronger. If money is tied to your self-worth, that can be a major problem. Money matters often complicate one's state of affairs rather than make things easier, especially if you use money to control others. Discuss your attitude toward money before marriage. If there's a problem, be sure it's solved before you decide to walk down the aisle together. Later may be too late.

 **Sid's Wisdom:** If you encounter a major financial strain, you and your spouse can still maintain a good relationship by filling up your "love account" with patience, kindness, and concern for each other.

*"Life affords no greater responsibility, no greater privilege, than the raising of the next generation."*

—C. Everett Koop

# *Starting a Family*

The wish to have children is inherent in the majority of couples who decide to marry. However, there are those who either want to delay having children or, actually, don't want children at all. It's important to discuss this issue prior to marriage so there won't be any future misunderstandings. Think what a shame it would be if you didn't discuss it, got married, and then found out that one of you was fixed with the idea not to have children while the other person had a strong desire to raise a family. This is a major difference that would surely jeopardize your marriage, and one not easily resolved at a later date.

The desire to have a family is a completely natural inclination. But make no mistake about it—having a child will change the dynamics of the relationship. Much of your energy will be taken up in parenting them. Raising children is no easy task, especially if you find yourself plagued with memories of your own childhood that you don't want them to repeat. On the other hand, nurturing a family can be one of the most joyous and rewarding experiences of your life. If children are to be part of your future, ask yourself what you have to offer them. If the answer is love, happiness, and a bright future, then you're on the right track.

# Do You Have Good Reasons for Wanting to Have Children?

The decision to start a family is a big step in any marriage, and most couples will decide to have their first child at some point. In every way, it's a natural extension of their love for one another—or so it should be viewed. Unfortunately, this is not always the case. Difficult as it is to believe, some people resort to having a child as a cure-all for a marriage in trouble. However, this seldom serves to save a marriage. More important, think about how unfair this is to the child. No couple should agree to have children unless their own relationship is a healthy one.

I've known couples who, prior to marriage, talked about having children, and one or both of them expressed the view that they didn't want to have any. Some have changed their minds and ended up having a family for one reason or another. Perhaps it was to add another dimension to their marriage, to leave a legacy, or to raise a child who would take over a family business.

Most parents see having a child as the most important part of their marriage. To them, children represent the extension of their own existence—created in their own image, growing, learning, and becoming responsible adults.

Whatever your reasons for wanting to have children, go into it with your eyes fully open. Realize that it's your responsibility to provide your children with the support and opportunities they'll need to flourish as worthy individuals.

**Sid's Wisdom:** When couples enter into marriage, most aren't educated in the job of parenting. They'll most likely learn by doing. As you enter into marriage, take a pledge to each other that you'll together make every effort possible to create a loving, caring, and secure home for your children.

## When Should You Start a Family and How Many Children Would You Like to Have?

When you come to an agreement to have children, you'll want to discuss when to have your first child and what size family you'd like. It's often wise to put off having children until you've had some time to yourselves and you know your marriage is on solid ground, especially if you're a young couple. Raising children is an ongoing responsibility of eighteen to twenty or more years, depending on how many children you have and how they're spaced in age. Once children enter the picture, much of your time and energy will be taken up with their needs, such as attending their school activities, sharing your values and, when necessary, disciplining them.

Equally important is agreeing on the number of children you want. If you grew up as an only child, can you even imagine a household with five or six little ones running around? I've spoken to a number of couples who fantasized about having a big family, and for most of them that's what it ended up being—a far-out fantasy. After having two or three children, they stopped because they came to realize how much work it involved. (Incidentally, you might want to give thought to having a few more candlelight dinners and taking in a few more movies before the curtain falls on your time alone.)

 **Sid's Wisdom:** Give thought to whether children will be or even should be a part of your future. Make sure you and your spouse-to-be share the same commitment to having a family. Nowhere in your marriage vows does it say you must have children. But millions of couples will tell you that your marriage is so much more rewarding if you do.

# What Is Your Approach to the Discipline of Children?

A discussion of your attitude toward disciplining children should take place before marriage. Take a look back at your own childhood and recall how you felt when you were disciplined. How were you punished as a child? Were rules imposed?

How you were treated by your parents may influence your decisions about your own children. If you find that your approach to disciplining children varies greatly from your future mate's, take the time to see if the two of you can agree on a common method that serves the best interest of the child. In many families, a child is never spanked. In others, spanking is considered acceptable and just.

Children become confused if parents aren't consistent in their method of discipline. If the rules are discussed in advance, children are then prepared to accept the consequences if they step out of line. It becomes their responsibility to live within the rules.

Children need continual guidance. When they make wrong choices in their lives, you as parents will have to deal with them. It can be frustrating and even anger-provoking at times. Make sure you, as parents, stick to nonabusive guidelines when it comes to the way you handle such difficulties. In most cases, a gentle, loving hand will bring better results. Screaming or verbal or physical abuse should never be tolerated.

 **Sid's Wisdom:** Children learn by example. Make your examples good ones.

# How Will You Share the Responsibility of Raising Children?

Which one of you will be the most involved with the children and their upbringing? For the early formative years, it's usually the wife who carries the responsibility for taking care of the children until their school years. Normally, the husband is the primary earner, and the need for a guaranteed income is extremely important with the increased costs of a child. This doesn't necessarily have to be the case, but it usually is. If a husband wishes to take on the responsibility of child raising, the matter should be discussed and the final decision arrived at by a consensus of both parents. Regardless, both should be involved in the raising of children. Each should set aside time to be with the children, oversee their ongoing needs, help with their homework, etc. A sense of family results from letting the children know they're loved, that their wants and needs are right up there with the needs of the family, and that their opinions and talents are welcomed and appreciated.

 **Sid's Wisdom:** Compatibility within a family begins the moment a child is born. If children feel loved and important to the family, they'll want to remain a part of the family for the remainder of their lives.

# Do You Realize the Tremendous Commitment Involved in Bringing Up Children?

Having children should unify a couple and strengthen the relationship. Prior to having children, it's much easier to contemplate divorce because there are only the two of you who will be affected by the separation. When there are children, the need for a mother and father is critical. In the United States today, the divorce rate is more than 50 percent, and a majority are in families who have children. The number of problem children in one-parent families is exceedingly high. It's so important that those of you who contemplate marriage recognize your responsibility to the children you bring into the world and make every effort to ensure that your marriage will be a long-term commitment.

Why should children have to suffer because of unfortunate decisions of their parents before they're born? Children can, and will, bring enrichment to your marriage. Don't bring them into a family where there's constant bickering and unhappiness. Children are a source of love and pride. Make sure you both want to bring children into your lives.

 **Sid's Wisdom:** Children are a result of your love for one another. Make sure you save a slice of that love for them as well.

## How Would You Feel About Adopting a Child?

Adopting a child can be one of the most rewarding experiences of your life. Children available for adoption who need a stable and loving home environment include American babies, children from other countries, children with special needs, and overlooked older children. Adoption today is easier to accomplish than in years past as many of the requirements traditionally associated with it such as minimal salary standards (which were set very high), home ownership, physical handicaps, sexual preference, and even marriage no longer apply.

The adoption process can be frustrating, emotionally difficult, and time-consuming. There are literally thousands of agencies, both public and private, that can help in the process. Finding a qualified and ethical one is the key. Independent adoption—adoption arranged without an agency—is legal in all but a few states. If you pursue this approach, you should retain an experienced adoption attorney to explain the adoption laws in your state.

Whether you want to adopt because you can't have children of your own or because you have a desire to provide otherwise parentless children with a caring home, educate yourselves and explore all the issues inherent in the adoption process. Be sure you're both reaching for the same dream and have the resources to attain your desired goal, for the sake of all.

 **Sid's Wisdom:** If you're thinking of adopting a child, talk with other parents who have adopted children. They'll let you know what to expect on a journey you'll never forget.

# *Religion and Other Spiritual Matters*

For thousands of years, religion has played an important role in the decision to marry. It is easy and foolhardy to just say, "We love each other, that's all that matters," and move blissfully on, ignoring religious differences. From the very moment you begin to plan your wedding, religion can be a major issue, from the wedding service to how you raise your children, especially if you're of different faiths. With discussion and a little foresight, love and understanding can conquer all when issues that have to do with religious practices arise.

Aside from the wedding ceremony, discuss religion and spiritual matters in advance as they relate to attending one or the other's place of worship, raising children in your religion, how religious holidays will be celebrated, and the many moral and spiritual issues within the family. Some individuals have been raised mainly within a religious "family"—their friends have been religious friends and their social and philanthropic activities have centered around their place of worship. Other people have had little exposure to organized religion. What is important is that each person in the marriage be able to freely continue his or her spiritual beliefs and practices. As private a matter as religion may be to you or to your potential spouse, discussing its effect on your ongoing relationship is extremely important.

# How Big a Role Do You Think Religion Should Play in Your Lives?

For some people, organized religion is a major part of their lives—reading the sacred texts, attending services, singing in the choir, and participating in various religious functions. For others, religious practice is seldom of concern.

When you sit down to talk about your wedding plans, this issue will no doubt arise. After all, one of the first things to decide is whether to have a religious ceremony, and if so, where. In the meantime, religion is an issue that should be fully discussed long before walking down the aisle. For example, what traditions will you follow? Will you say grace at mealtimes? Will you attend your house of worship daily, weekly, or just on religious holidays? How much money will you contribute yearly to your religious organization? Will you celebrate religious holidays with other family members and friends? Are there activities or practices that one partner's religion allows which the other's forbids?

As you and your future spouse discuss the role of religion in your lives, be sure you understand fully each other's expectations.

**Sid's Wisdom:** When you and your future spouse talk about religious faith and spirituality, you'll gain insights into each other as individuals. You may find that it brings you closer together in many unforeseen ways.

# Is It Important That Your Spouse Be Spiritually Oriented?

This question is different from the one having to do with specific religious faiths and what church you attend. This has to do with your inner life and the guidance you seek there. It's about the highly personal relationship you have within yourself to a higher divinity or supreme being—what many people call God or Buddha or Gaia, the life-force of Nature itself.

If you're a highly spiritual person—for instance, one who prays or meditates daily—and you marry someone who has no interest in spiritual matters, you most likely will encounter trouble in your marriage. Two people from different religions who are comfortable with the differences will most likely have a better chance for a happy marriage than two people who are totally opposite in their spiritual orientation and intolerant of each other's stance.

 **Sid's Wisdom:** For those seeking a higher spiritual self, it is best to marry a kindred spirit. There's no lack of spiritual-seekers in today's world.

# Will Differences Over Religious Beliefs Become an Issue in Your Marriage?

If you and your partner are of different faiths or different spiritual beliefs, will it get in the way of a harmonious marriage? Or will you respect each other's religious practices and spiritual beliefs and allow each other the right to express those practices and beliefs in the way you individually deem fit?

If your concept of God is different from your mate's, explore the various insights each of you has regarding how faith and God manifest themselves in your lives. You may find more of a meeting of the minds than you had imagined. Whatever your beliefs, there no doubt will be times in your marriage when you'll struggle with some of them. Will you and your partner be supportive of each other when facing these problems? There will always be questions of faith such as "Why aren't my prayers being answered?" or "How could God let this happen to me?" These questions may all have a familiar ring, and there are many more that may arise.

In addition to these issues, you should ask if your loved one's concept of life after death is different from yours. Have you discussed dealing with the death of a family member or close friend? Have you let your partner know your own religious preferences in case of serious illness, injury, or death? Do you know the desires of your partner? Although these are not issues that arise often in a marriage, they're questions that need to be discussed at an early point.

**Sid's Wisdom:** Your attitude toward religion and spiritual beliefs can be pivotal in making the decision to marry. If you're religiously inclined or not, get it out in the open early in your relationship. Later may be too late!

## What Are Your Views about Your Children's Religious Upbringing?

If children enter your marriage, it's important that you and your spouse have a mutual understanding of how you'll introduce them to spiritual matters. Parents who have strong religious beliefs will want their children to attend their place of worship with them as soon as they can and possibly enroll them in a religious-based school. The opportunities to involve children depend upon the practices of the religious organization in question. As children mature, they'll form attitudes of their own about religious affiliations. They may remain content with their religious experiences, or they may want to move on to other religious experiences and opportunities. Are you both prepared to accept such decisions? How would you deal with them?

In what faith, if any, will your children be raised? Will your children attend religious services? Will they attend a religious school? What religious holidays will be celebrated? Discuss before marriage your attitudes toward your children-to-be, if any, and their religious upbringing. It is helpful for you and your partner to look back on your own introduction to religion and consider how it has affected your lives.

**Sid's Wisdom:** You can offer your children your advice and experience in religious matters as guidelines, but recognize that the final decision must be their own.

*"A marriage without conflicts is almost as inconceivable as a nation without crises."*
**—André Maurois**

# *Extended Family and Friends – In-Laws and Outlaws*

When marrying, consideration should be given in advance to what your mutual relationships will be with each other's families and close friends. Couples generally want to be accepted and get along with their in-laws and their future mate's long-time friends, but sometimes this is more easily said than done. There are all kinds of in-laws and friends out there—some more meddlesome than others, some more supportive than others.

When you marry, you inherit your in-laws and your partner's close friends, regardless of your true feelings about them. As a certain amount of inspection of you as the future spouse is common, patience may be required. You, too, will want to get to know your future relatives on a more intimate level, find out what they enjoy doing, what they expect of you, what their hopes are for your marriage. Open and honest communication is the key to starting out on the right foot with your extended family!

In-laws and close friends will play some part in your married life, whether you like it or not. The moment you announce your marriage, they'll have expectations of that marriage and advice to give. It may be in your best interest to listen, for you never know what you can glean from their questions and suggestions. On the other hand, you and your future spouse may need to set some boundaries when it comes to extended family and friends. The questions in this section will help you better determine this.

# Will You Get Along with Each Other's Family and Friends?

When you start talking about a wedding date, you'll want to celebrate your marriage with the full support of each other's family and friends. Full support doesn't mean only on the day of the wedding ceremony, but for the duration of your marriage—which is to last a lifetime.

Inheriting a family and a group of friends along with the person you have come to love may take some adaptation. At first you may feel as if you've been placed under a microscope or are being dissected on the lab table—a painful process indeed! Take a deep breath, keep an open mind, and trust that eventually everyone will relax around one another. If all goes well, you'll be friends forever.

If, however, time passes and you don't feel comfortable with your future mother-in-law or some of your beloved's friends, it's no use pretending that you find them wonderful and accepting of you. Hang in there. They say love conquers all; this may be a good place to start.

Discuss your concerns with your future mate. She may have insights and answers you haven't thought of that will alleviate some of your concerns.

**Sid's Wisdom:** It's impossible to have a perfect life. If there's someone among your future spouse's family or friends who may create problems, don't spend a lot of time fretting about it. Try and accept the situation and move on to more positive things.

# Are There Concerns You Should Be Aware of Regarding Your Intended's Family and Possible Unforeseen Commitments?

As much as you would like to think that the two of you are going to get married and be entirely on your own, family situations may arise that you can't just walk away from. These might include a financial disaster hitting a close family member, a parent becoming seriously ill, or a sudden death in the family. Any kind of unforeseen event such as this could affect your marriage. For example, if you live far away from the relative or in-law concerned, your spouse may find it necessary to spend time away from you to assist with the needs of that person. She may even encourage you to pick up and move to the same area in the event constant care is needed. Would you be prepared to do this?

I know a man who, shortly after marrying, insisted on moving his mother into the couple's home, because she was distraught when her husband was killed in a car accident. This placed a great strain on the couple's marriage. Discuss what you might do in the face of such a catastrophe.

In almost everyone's lifetime, there are situations that require family members to participate in a support process. When such situations occur, most couples aren't properly prepared to communicate their feelings about how to deal with the circumstances. This may upset their relationship and make things more difficult than they need to be, for both parties.

**Sid's Wisdom:** In any family emergency, you need to keep a level head as a couple, and think things through as clearly as possible. Listen to each other's concerns, and be supportive and considerate of one another.

# Do You Have Friends in Common?

It's easy to get so wrapped up in your relationship that you isolate yourselves from your friends. This is particularly true when your relationship is new and developing and Cupid's arrow has had its effect. In time, however, you'll probably want to introduce each other to your respective friends. You hope the people you've spent time with in the past will measure up to the expectations of your mate-to-be. In turn, you'll be able to tell much about your future spouse by the company he keeps.

If you get along with your future spouse's closest friends and start spending time with them, they might reveal some eye-opening things about him you didn't know. But then, what are friends for? Hopefully, they'll also be able to share some of their wonderful memories and funny stories with you.

It's never too late to reestablish bonds of friendship. So even if you've lost touch for a while, get back in touch. Friends are an important part of a full and happy life.

**Sid's Wisdom:** Good mutual friends can add joyous moments to your life and to the success of your marriage.

# How Will You Be Affected Knowing That Your Intended Has Many Friends of the Opposite Sex?

Do you know your future partner well enough to know if he's inclined to make friends with or already has many women friends? If this applies to your relationship, inwardly you may want to determine if you're jealous or comfortable with it. You don't necessarily want to end up trying to cut those friends out of his life, nor will you want to feel the need to control those friendships.

There are two ways the above scenario can play out. If your instincts tell you he truly enjoys having women friends and it's just friendship, that's fine. But beware of the guy who thinks there's always something more exciting than you around the corner. This kind of thinking can lead to presumed friendships becoming affairs. If you've gone so far as to consider marriage together, this probably will not be the case. Talk with some of his male friends. They may enlighten you as to his relationships with women.

It's not uncommon today for partners in a marriage to have friends of the opposite sex who they occasionally have lunch with, work out with, or share other activities that their spouses aren't interested in. However, these activities should take place when the married couples wouldn't be spending time together (dinnertime or evenings) and shouldn't include drinking or partying.

 **Sid's Wisdom:** If you feel anxious about the friendships your future mate has with the opposite sex, talk candidly with each other about your feelings. Perhaps there's nothing to fear but fear itself.

# *Are You Still Friends with a Former Lover?*

Unless this is your first true close relationship, chances are you may still have ties with boyfriends or girlfriends from the past. Are there unresolved issues with the past? For instance, if you were terribly hurt by a former girlfriend or boyfriend, have you forgiven that person in your heart, or are you still carrying around guilt and/or resentment? If so, you're already jeopardizing the relationship with the person you now intend to marry. The memory of an ex-lover can provoke all kinds of emotions—from friendship to intense dislike. If you have hurtful ongoing feelings relating to past romantic relationships, get them out in the open, resolve them, and move forward with your new life.

Love can be painful. You know this from the time you got your first crush on someone. The way you processed your disappointments and mistakes is what's important. If you're planning to marry someone who is still friends with an ex-lover, you can learn a lot about your future mate by paying attention to how they relate.

This also applies to ex-spouses. They can remain friends regardless of their previous relationship. How will you deal with this? Will it make you feel uncomfortable or insecure? Have such discussions with your mate-to-be early on if you feel it's important.

Honest and open discussions are an important part of marriage. Try not to allow things from your past to negatively affect your marriage. A happy future is your primary goal.

**Sid's Wisdom:** The best way to learn about previous relationships is to talk about them. But open this door with caution. Endless discussions about past issues might present misunderstandings and have an adverse effect on your relationship.

## What If You Don't Like Each Other's Choice of Friends?

It's possible that certain of your friends may be unlikable or even unacceptable to your mate. There may be personality conflicts, few interests in common, objectionable personal habits, or jealousy stemming from the past. Whatever the case, be frank about your feelings toward each other's friends.

Perhaps your partner isn't comfortable about a friendship you have with someone of the opposite sex. Maybe you get irritated when he spends too much time with his friends. If you can talk openly about problems such as these, you'll get a more accurate reading on your partner and your relationship in general.

I've met many couples who have had to make compromises with respect to their outside friendships. One woman in particular was aghast at the behavior of her mate's best friend. Every time she saw him, he was boisterous and crude. She couldn't understand how anyone could stand to be around this person and she avoided him! However, as she got to know him better, she realized he had one of the biggest hearts around.

Eventually, they became good friends. Sometimes it's just a matter of keeping an open mind and giving time to the situation when it comes to your mate's choice of friends.

I've also known partners who for one reason or another have destroyed a long-standing friendship of their mate's. This usually hinders a couple's relationship more than it helps. If you truly can't stand a close friend of your future spouse, let him know you don't want to spend time with that person, but you won't stand in the way of their continuing the friendship if it doesn't affect your marriage.

 **Sid's Wisdom:** True friends understand that relationships can change when a spouse enters the picture, and they make allowances for this new relationship in their friend's life.

*"Marriage should be a duet—when one sings, the other claps."*

**—Source Unknown**

# Common Interests

Discovering what interests you have in common is crucial to a healthy and happy marriage. There are many kinds of activities you can explore together—sports, music, art, travel, exercise, and hobbies, to name a few. Doing things together in areas of mutual interest may be the most rewarding hours you'll share.

If you don't have shared interests, problems can arise in your marriage. We've all heard of couples who split up simply because they "grew apart." Chances are that the couple didn't explore the vast opportunities available for having fun together. It's good for each person in a marriage to have interests outside the family, but they shouldn't become so time consuming that mutual interests are overlooked.

Too often, couples get stuck in a rut doing the same things together, such as going to the movies—where there's no interaction—or being constantly together with friends—which presents little opportunity for intimacy. Life is full of surprises, and sometimes the little things you do together bring surprising discoveries about your loved one and enhance your relationship. For example, let's say you're taking a walk in the woods and your significant other starts identifying all the trees and native shrubs in the area. What an unexpected surprise that would be.

# Is There a Hobby That You and Your Fiancé Both Enjoy or Could Develop an Interest In?

Hobbies can run the gamut from stamp collecting to old train sets, from bird watching to puzzles. Does one or both of you have a hobby that you could pursue together? Why not give each other a short list of fun hobbies you could do together and take turns picking one? Try them out until you reach an agreement on the one or more hobbies that appeal to both of you. A shared hobby can provide you with ongoing opportunities to improve certain skills, meet interesting people, and gain knowledge. For example, you could join a writer's group and hone your writing skills or participate in an investment club where you learn about what stocks to invest in. Many couples have met each other at these kinds of get-togethers, and their shared hobbies continue to bring significant pleasure to their relationship.

 **Sid's Wisdom:** If you look at the kinds of hobbies you can share, you'll probably find many possibilities. Hobbies are a way of sharing quality time together and they can help prevent a marriage from going stale.

# Do You Have a Favorite Sport or Physical Activity You Like to Participate In?

Keeping healthy and physically fit has become a passion for many people today. Much of staying fit revolves around outdoor sports and activities like swimming, tennis, bicycling, volleyball, and hiking, or joining a gym and working out on machines or taking aerobics classes.

Do you and your partner have the same level of commitment to exercise and living a healthy lifestyle? Keeping fit is a lot easier and more fun when you have someone you can work out or jog with. There are many other activities and sports you can do together as well that will keep you in each other's company and enjoying the time you spend together. Dancing is a great form of exercise that allows you to, literally, stay in touch.

If sports and strenuous exercise aren't your thing, but you know how important it is to your loved one, let him enjoy keeping fit on his own. You may prefer a gentle yoga class or a daily walk, and he, in turn, should encourage you to do what you enjoy. Couples need freedom to pursue separate interests as well as shared ones.

**Sid's Wisdom:** If you find yourselves worlds apart when it comes to physical activity, try to find an environment where you can still be together but doing your own thing. For instance, the beach is a place where one of you can swim or play volleyball and the other just relax and read.

# How Will Television Affect Your Time Together?

In today's world, television seems to have captured the after dinner and weekend hours in most households. Is this how you'll choose to spend your precious time together after you're married? Do you know if your significant other plans to sit glued to the boob tube every night? If he does, do you expect him to change this habit when you begin living under the same roof?

Granted, many of us have a favorite show we wouldn't want to miss. But constant television viewing can doom your marriage because it doesn't allow for conversation between the two of you. It can close you off to discussing things of mutual importance. If one of you is always tuned in to the TV, it may make the other feel tuned out.

Television will probably play some part in your marriage, but it's important to sit down in advance and discuss how much television viewing will be acceptable to both of you and which shows you might watch together or separately.

 **Sid's Wisdom:** Make it clear to your loved one that you would rather spend quality time with her than sit in front of the television every night—even if it means missing some of your favorite shows. You'll score more than a few points on this one!

# Do You Enjoy Reading?

Do you envision quiet evenings curled up on the sofa with your beloved reading and discussing your favorite books, only to find out that your future spouse has never read a book? This could provide you with quite a jolt, but the truth of the matter is that women buy and read more books than men. I once spoke with a well-read woman whose fiancé seemed to know a lot about everything, so she assumed that he was an avid reader—and he was, of magazines. It's all he ever read; he had never in his life picked up a book. She was so disappointed knowing this that she broke off the relationship.

If reading is important in your life, you need to know if your future spouse feels the same. Being able to share and talk about the books, stories, and articles you read is one of life's pleasures and can add to the quality of your relationship. If you're not a reader, you may feel left out when your beloved gets involved in a good book and ignores you for periods of time.

 **Sid's Wisdom:** Browsing in a bookstore with your loved one can shed light on their particular interests and propensity for reading.

# Minor versus Major Issues, or What Kind of Music Do You Like?

It's surprising how many minor differences become apparent when couples get married and start living together. One of the differences that may arise is an opposite taste in music. Unless you spend a great deal of time with one another in each other's home environment, you may not be aware that your partner likes loud rock music blaring both day and night. You prefer soft rock and smooth jazz at lower decibels. This simple difference could become a regular disagreement between you.

Most conflict occurs over these kinds of minor disagreements. Learning to manage your conflicts is a skill you need to develop before you marry. Even if you don't yet know what all your differences are, this is an important skill to develop. For instance, if you have an ongoing conflict about the music issue, how will you compromise to keep the peace? Will you honor your partner's right to feel the way he does about his music? Will you listen carefully to his side and try to understand where he's coming from? Will you have an attitude of give and take during your discussions? When you do come to a compromise, will you be able to appreciate your partner's efforts? If so, you can safely assume that you'll have taken the first step to a lasting marriage.

**Sid's Wisdom:** When unresolved minor disagreements pile up in a relationship, you can be sure you're entering into a risky marriage. If this is the case, you should consider postponing the marriage until you can work things through via a loving compromise.

# Do You Like to Travel?

Travel is one of those things where if you don't have the right companion, it can be disappointing. Have you and your mate-to-be taken trips together? Were you trapped in the car with a virtual lunatic whose only thought was to reach his destination, while you would have liked to stop and smell the roses along the way? Or maybe you flew together for a weekend to visit relatives and she turned out to be a white-knuckle flyer who complained during the entire flight. She vowed never to fly again—and you wondered if that meant you'd be skipping the honeymoon plans in the Caribbean. Or maybe you grew up taking camping trips with friends and family and the thought of doing this with your beloved seems romantic to you, but she just wants to know if there will be room service available.

If one of you has a burning desire to travel and the other has no interest, will you be able to reach a compromise? For example, when vacation time rolls around and you're looking forward to an adventure away from home but your partner would prefer to stick around the house and repair some things that need fixing, how will you handle that?

Traveling can be a wonderful sharing and learning experience. Spend some time talking about how you feel about travel, what your past experiences have been, and how you would see yourselves traveling in the future. Talk about places you'd like to visit. What are your views of family trips? We've all heard the traumatic tales of traveling with children. All of life is an adventure. Hopefully, your vacations can and will provide you both with many pleasures.

**Sid's Wisdom:** Prior to marriage, be sure that taking trips is something you'll enjoy doing together. It might be a good idea to take some short excursions to determine if you'll be happy in this area of your marriage.

## *Would You Mind Having a Pet in the House?*

Perhaps you grew up in a household with pets, but your intended never even had the goldfish experience. Now that you're considering marriage, she wonders what you intend to do with your feline and canine friends. Of course, you're attached to them, but how attached are you? Would you be willing to give them up because your future wife is allergic and won't even permit them in her house? Having pets in the home is a subject that can cause major disagreements. Maybe it won't be an issue with just the two of you, but if you plan to have children, you can bet the time will come when they'll want a kitten or a puppy or some other creature that requires daily care and feeding. It's better to sort this out now so you'll know where you both stand. Children are often relentless about this issue.

Having pets can make it difficult to find housing. Many owners don't sanction having them on their property. Even if they do allow pets, having a large dog in a small space can create a problem. On the other hand, giving up a devoted pet can be quite emotional. One solution might be to give the animal temporarily to a close friend who will allow you visitation rights. Be prepared though—the dog that was once your constant companion may become your friend's best friend! Then what do you do?

 **Sid's Wisdom:** If you have a pet you can't bear to give up, think of it this way: whose warm body would you rather have next to you in bed each night?

## Do You Like to Cook?

Perhaps you delighted in whipping up gourmet dishes for your beloved during the courtship feeding time, but are you prepared to continue cooking countless meals after you're married? Following marital bliss, mealtime becomes the most shared experience in a majority of homes. Even though most families today don't share three meals every day, try to sit down together for at least one.

Although some women still consider the kitchen their territory, it's more and more becoming part of a husband's domain as well. What a relief, no doubt—or is it! This is mainly because of the changing lifestyles of married couples and the dual working situations, which bring into focus the need for sharing household responsibilities.

Many women find it enjoyable to have their mate in the kitchen sharing the culinary experience. Indeed, one woman I spoke to makes it a prerequisite once every weekend that her husband prepare a meal. Whatever arrangement you work out, dinner is the principal time of the day when you and your partner can still put a little romance on the front burner and share the happenings of your day.

**Sid's Wisdom:** If one of the problems you foresee with your potential spouse is that he doesn't like to cook, agree that he sets the table and does the dishes. You may suggest that you take a cooking class together. Many adult education schools offer them. It's also a place to socialize and meet new friends with a common interest. After all, everyone has to eat!

## *Do You Like to Socialize and Entertain at Home?*

The way you relate in social situations, how you interact with others, and your overall comfort level about socializing have a lot to do with your personality type. Are you and your intended both outgoing types? Are you both warm and friendly? Is your level of sophistication about the same? The amount and type of social involvement preferred by you and your prospective mate is an important issue to be discussed BEFORE marriage. What are your expectations when it comes to the amount of entertaining you'll do in your home? Does your mate have a lot of friends he or she likes to spend time with? Are you comfortable with Sunday afternoon barbecues in your backyard? Every Sunday?

While dating, you and your prospective spouse are most often on your best behavior, trying to impress one another. Here's a common scenario: Richard and Janet have just met. Janet loves to cook for her friends and she holds lavish dinner parties often. During their entire courtship, Richard is happy to attend Janet's parties. He's cordial to all the guests (her friends), can hold his own in a conversation, and they have good times together. Once married, however, things change. Richard announces he doesn't feel comfortable entertaining so often in their new home. He wants more privacy. Now when they're invited out to parties, Richard often refuses to go. Suddenly, he doesn't like her friends so well. Janet becomes despondent and feels like a prisoner in her own home.

Had Janet known all this before she and Richard married, they might have been able to make some compromises early on. However, in their case, it was too late. This is precisely why it's so important to make sure you and your partner share a compatible social style.

**Sid's Wisdom:** Be sincere and up front with your mate about your attitude toward socializing. If you find that one of you likes to socialize more than the other, allow that person to enjoy an occasional event outside the home (with or without you) and also to be able to entertain friends in the home from time to time.

# Do You Value Individual Interests and Time to Yourself?

As important as it is in a marriage to have common interests, it's equally important to have individual interests and some time to yourselves. Time apart can mean that you like to spend an occasional evening cooking a gourmet meal with your girlfriends, or that your mate likes to get together with his friends on Saturday mornings to shoot a few hoops. Separate hobbies can provide you with the opportunity to learn and experience different things that renew your individual spirits—so that when you're together, you have more to give to each other. It helps keep your relationship alive and interesting.

Spending quiet moments alone gives you time to reflect on your innermost thoughts, which is important for keeping a feeling of oneness with yourself. Aside from your marriage, the most important relationship you have is with yourself, and unless it's a satisfying one, what can you expect to have to share with others—especially your ever-loving lifetime mate?

 **Sid's Wisdom:** Periodically, give yourself and your loved one space to be alone and to pursue separate interests. It's part of the glue that keeps a marriage together. Marriage is about trust and feeling comfortable with one another, whether you're side by side or away from each other for intervals of time.

171

# Personal Habits—Those Finicky Domestic Things

There's an old adage that it's easier to learn a new good habit than break an old bad one. Everyone has good and bad habits learned over the years from one's parents, siblings, and friends. Sometimes we're unaware of our little personal habits that in a marriage may bother our mate and others on a grand scale.

When you're dating or "in love," you have a tendency to overlook the bad habits of your significant other. But when you're spending twenty-four hours a day together, those habits can become a source of irritation that may drive you crazy. Dirty laundry left on the floor once in a while may not annoy you, but a continual lack of interest in keeping the house neat and tidy, dirty clothes washed, the lawn mowed, and other unanswered problems may bring about more than just mild anger. There are other habits that could drive you up the wall as well—poor table manners, smoking, drinking, foul language, the list goes on and on!

Some habits may be difficult to discover before you live together. I have a friend who got married and had no idea her husband had an aversion to the bedroom window being open during the night. They had many arguments about it until they finally resolved it with the following scenario each evening upon retiring: She would open the window before climbing into bed. He would come in and close the window. After he fell asleep, she would get up and open it again. Sometime during the night, he would awaken, climb out of bed and close it. It seems they spent more time out of bed than in bed!

There are some personal habits of your loved one you may not be able to change. You may just have to accept them. This is true in most marriages. When someone brings happiness into your life that you've never experienced before, little things can and should be overlooked, because you come to realize that, in the long run, the benefits outweigh the deficits. A marriage without differences could be extremely boring.

# Are You a Finicky Eater?

There's no accounting for taste buds, and yet eating is a daily occurrence. Most families eat three meals a day. If you and your intended come from different ethnic backgrounds, your food choices and eating habits may be very different. Agreeing on what meals to cook and eat on a daily basis can be tricky. This is why it's important prior to marriage to find out about each other's likes and dislikes when it comes to the meals you'll eat. To pretend you like something you really dislike almost guarantees that you'll find it on your plate again and again!

Today's consumer-oriented food world has made it easier to prepare meals. Your local markets offer a greater array of healthy food selections. Still, you want to be sure you're on the same wavelength as your partner. Get questions answered like: Do you have any dietary restrictions? Are you allergic to any particular food? Do you have any favorite dishes? Do you like to eat out often or occasionally? Be open to your mate's suggestions and be willing to sample new dishes and try out new recipes. Many of the seemingly strange aromas and flavorings you're not accustomed to in time may become favorites. "Try it, you might like it" is relevant here.

 **Sid's Wisdom:** When possible, make menu planning and grocery shopping a joint effort. This ensures that both partners have the opportunity to select some of the foods and snacks they each enjoy.

# What Are Your Sleeping Habits?

Imagine the following plight: You've lived alone and slept soundly through the night for years. Now you're getting married to a wonderful partner who is considerate and cares about your every need—only he's an insomniac and likes to read in bed for most of the night. Or he often falls asleep with the television on. Suddenly, you find yourself not getting enough rest and you become irritable. Sleepless nights are taking a toll on your marriage.

Perhaps you get married and then find out that your spouse snores. You spend long nights poking him in the ribs to get him to stop. This becomes an irritating problem in your marriage. You both desperately seek solutions. A friend tells you to sew a big cork into the outside yoke of his pajama top to prevent him from sleeping on his back. You consider wearing earplugs or sleeping in the spare bedroom as a last resort. And you thought love could conquer all—but now you're not so sure.

When problems arise in your marriage, work together for a solution. In the case of a heavy snorer, seek medical advice. If it's not diagnosed as a serious problem, it can sometimes be helped through daily exercise or elevating the upper body and head while sleeping. Whatever it takes, try it! There's nothing worse than losing sleep over the shut-eye habits of your spouse.

 **Sid's Wisdom:** If you're not aware of your future spouse's sleeping habits, you should find out by talking about them to eliminate unexpected surprises.

# Do You Have Any Unhealthy or Harmful Habits?

You may already know that your fiancé smokes, drinks, or gambles occasionally, but you may not know the extent of such habits. If there's any question in your mind about them, speak to his family and friends to find out if he has a history of heavy drinking, taking drugs, or a problem with quitting smoking or gambling. Smoking and gambling are addictions that are extremely hard to break. Gambling and alcoholism, especially, can ruin a marriage. Many men and women are in denial about their alcohol problems. Others have an uncanny knack of hiding their problem. Hopefully, your future spouse isn't hiding any secrets such as these from you.

If you do discover that your fiancé has a history of alcoholism, gambling, or taking drugs, speak openly and honestly about it. Perhaps he's on the road to recovery and is deserving of your support. On the other hand, if the problem continues to exist, don't expect such habits to change overnight. Your loved one needs a qualified counselor to help him cure his addiction. Inform your fiancé that if and when he finds a cure, you may reconsider marriage.

 **Sid's Wisdom:** Unhealthy and harmful habits are often a sign of deeper problems. Permanent changes don't come about easily. Let him know you'll continue to be his friend, but marriage is out of the question until recovery is complete.

# What Is Your Attitude Toward Table Manners?

How many of us were brought up by parents who, at the dinner table, constantly reproached us for our poor table manners? Often heard were the words, "Boys, sit up straight and use your fork properly!" I'm sure many of you can relate to this.

In some households, it may have been improper to reach across the table for a biscuit. In others, reaching across the table was never an issue. A lot of this is cultural. For example, at the Chinese table all the food, except bowls of rice that are placed in front of each diner, is put in the middle of the table and everyone reaches for a serving with their chopsticks. No big deal! This might be unacceptable in another household. In many cultures, few words are spoken at the dinner table. It's mainly a place for nourishment. In other homes, the dinner table is a place for lively conversation, catching up with events of the day, and expressing whatever comes to mind. What would your preference be?

Can you imagine sitting across the table from someone for fifty years who slurps their soup, stuffs their mouth with huge amounts of food, and tries to talk at the same time? Maybe this wouldn't bother you, but others it would. Get in sync with each other on these issues before you marry. If you want your spouse to be able to set a table, it's important for them to know where to place the napkin, knife, fork, and spoon. Don't find fault with them. Show them and save them the embarrassment. Everyone has things to learn in life, so be considerate of your loved one in all instances.

**Sid's Wisdom:** Even if you have no interest in such mundane things as how to fold a dinner napkin, appreciate your soon-to-be partner for his or her attention to this kind of detail. It'll surely win you some points.

## How Will You Divide the Household Chores?

Marriage is intended to be a "sharing" experience. You share thoughts and ideas, happiness and sorrow—and you share responsibilities. If you both work, it's reasonable to assume that both of you will perform some of the household chores or you'll divide up the responsibilities according to who prefers to do what. There are so many everyday tasks to complete that if the burden falls on just one of you, resentment is bound to build up. In addition, there's nothing more aggravating than for your partner to have to constantly remind you to fulfill your obligations. Gone are the days when you can just walk through the door after a day's work, laze around, and ask, "When's dinner, babe?" If you do, don't be surprised if the response is, "Get real, buster!"

Sit down before you begin living under the same roof and draw up a list of all the things that need to be done on a daily, weekly, and monthly basis. You might include grocery shopping, cooking meals, feeding the pets, taking out the garbage, vacuuming, washing dishes, polishing furniture, doing laundry, making the bed, picking up dry cleaning, and washing windows. Then decide who has the pleasure of doing which task. You'll find that by figuring it out beforehand, your marriage will run into fewer troubles in this area.

**Sid's Wisdom:** As a married couple, it's important to live harmoniously, without a lot of bickering about who should do what. To this end, it helps not to focus on each other's faults. If your spouse neglects to carry out his or her end of the chores, don't go ballistic. Ease off, ask why, and try seeing things from his or her perspective. Don't let these things become a point of contention.

## Are You a Punctual Person or Are You Habitually Late for Engagements?

I know a couple who never arrives anywhere on time, regardless of their best intentions. Their friends have gotten wise and now specify a time to get there at least twenty minutes before the time they're actually expected. It works most of the time, but even then they're often late. Being late is considered inconsiderate by some and fashionable by others. What are your feelings about punctuality and being on schedule?

Nothing can be more irritating than waiting endlessly for your mate when you have a meeting or other appointment to get to. Whether you're a husband waiting for your spouse to get dressed to go out for the evening or a wife waiting for your husband to come home to an important dinner party you planned, being late can ruin the entire evening. If you're an on-time person about to marry someone who doesn't even own a watch, you'd better determine how problematic this might become.

When you enter into a relationship, you're often looking for someone who wants the same things you want, likes the same things you like, and who's going in the same direction in life—in other words, someone a lot like you. Hopefully, you'll find some of this in the person you're about to marry. But keep in mind that marriage also requires tolerance and acceptance of your differences.

 **Sid's Wisdom:** If you're an on-time person about to marry a person who's always late, look at it this way: You have a cause to conquer. Some form of compromise might come in handy here.

# How Will You Deal with Sharing a Bathroom?

Marriage presents many challenges to your daily living. Sharing a bathroom is one of them. For those of you who won't have to share a bathroom, I hope you realize how lucky you are! For those of you who will, you might as well know it now: There's no room in the house that can become a battleground faster than this small but important room. Vying for a little privacy in the morning can become a tug of war, especially when both of you are trying to get ready for work at the same time. Common complaints range from leaving wet towels on the floor to steaming up the mirror, not to mention leaving the toilet seat up and having the toilet paper roll out the wrong way.

Hundreds of letters have gone out to the Dear Abbys of the world trying to straighten out these seemingly minor problems. If you're sharing quarters for the first time, hopefully you can share the bathroom in a civilized way. At first, it may even seem exciting and sexy to see your naked partner standing beside you at the sink drying her hair. In time, however, after the newness of this experience wears away and she inadvertently blows your hairpiece off the top of your head (just kidding!), hopefully you'll look at it as laughable. All joking aside, are you prepared to adjust your habits or are you so set in your ways that you'll expect your partner to adjust their routine and habits to yours? If it's a small space, who's going to win?

 **Sid's Wisdom:** A schedule for the use of the bathroom can be worked out through a simple discussion of each other's needs. Being a good listener indicates respect for each other, and as a result, consideration for the other person takes priority.

# Are You a Morning Person or an Evening Person?

If you're accustomed to going to bed early and getting up at the crack of dawn but your significant other is a night owl, you may encounter some scheduling problems when you begin living together. This is where a willingness to compromise comes in handy. One of you may have to do without all the late-night movies you're in the habit of watching, or listening to loud music until the wee hours of the morning.

Getting used to one another's routines may take some time even after discussing your preferences in this often delicate area. If you're an early riser who leaps out of bed with boundless energy but your spouse likes to ease into the day slowly, you need to be considerate of each other's frame of mind during this time. For some people, reading the morning newspaper without a lot of interruptions is an essential part of their day. For others, getting to the gym or taking a jog before work is important. Whatever your particular habits are in the morning and before bedtime, discuss what's acceptable and not acceptable to your partner. One or both of you may find it possible to give up part of your routine to accommodate the other.

 **Sid's Wisdom:** Work on making some compromises in the areas where there may be differences. But have patience—some routines aren't always easily changed.

# Is Appearance Important to You?

For some people, appearance is everything—the way they dress, their manners, their degree of poise at social functions. Others could care less how they look on any occasion. How do you feel about this? It's an area where beauty may truly be in the eye of the beholder. If your potential spouse dresses in fashionable suits or clothing during the week but hangs around in tattered sweats on the weekends, would this be okay with you?

As you begin to spend time with your significant other attending various social events, it'll become apparent whether or not they dress appropriately. For example, if you're invited to a wedding where tuxedos are expected and your fiancé shows up in a forties pinstripe suit, would you feel comfortable? If not, don't start planning your own wedding with the thought that "Okay, I'll take care of that problem once we're married." No way! Who knows what he'll be wearing when he arrives at the altar!

The way your future spouse dresses may seem insignificant now, but look ahead to the future. I spoke to one young bride who, after being married for a year or so, was told by her husband that the disappointment for him in their marriage was the way she dressed. It wasn't sexy enough for him. She was totally taken aback, since he had never spoken a word about it before and, in fact, had given her many compliments regarding her wardrobe. The point is, if possible, take heed of these kinds of issues before you say "yes" to marriage. To one person it may be totally unimportant, to others extremely important. Why not find out now?

**Sid's Wisdom:** See each other in different kinds of environments, both socially and in more relaxed situations, to get a true idea of your future mate's attention to his or her appearance, both in manner of dress and social relationships. And if you think it's important, say something about it. It's better to know now how they'll react.

*"I dreamed of a wedding of elaborate elegance; a church filled with flowers and friends. I asked him what kind of wedding he wished for; he said one that would make me his wife."*
**—Source Unknown**

# The Wedding Plans

At last! You've made your way through 101 questions (or more!) and decided there are no hurdles high enough to keep you apart. You're meant for each other and are committing yourselves to a lifetime as husband and wife. Now comes the fun part—planning your wedding together. Will it be a big religious wedding with hundreds in attendance, or a simple ceremony in a beautiful garden? Or will you choose to elope and tie the knot on a beach on some exotic island? The most important part of planning your ceremony is that you make decisions that please both of you. Too many times, the groom takes an indifferent attitude toward wedding plans with an "I'll-wear-a-tie-and-tux-or-whatever-you-wish-dear" kind of response. I urge both parties to take an active part in the planning. You may be sorry if you don't.

There may be a thousand details to attend to before you find yourselves standing in front of whoever is going to marry you. Remember the in-laws you're about to inherit. And your own parents. No doubt they'll all want to have their say in many of those details. For example, you might hear these words: "All the women in our family have worn grandmother's wedding dress and you'd be offending all of us if you don't wear it." Forget about the fact that it's three sizes too big. Not a problem. Aunt Tilly can sew! Or what about these words: "Forget about this outdoor stuff! You should follow the family tradition and get married properly!"

My only and best words of advice to you are that your wedding should be tailored to what the two of you want, regardless of family pressures. By making this point clear from the very beginning, you may eliminate some of the family intervention that is likely to occur. Whatever you decide, you'll want to make it a special time that you can look back on fifty years from now and remember it as the most important moment of your lives.

# Sid's Closing Comments

## When married . . .

Never go to sleep at night without a kiss, regardless of any unhappiness between you. In the morning, you probably won't remember what it was you were unhappy about.

Plan at least one hour a week, and include all family members, to talk about anything that may be troubling you—vacation plans, things that have happened during the week, and so forth. Children are more likely to be family oriented if they're allowed to be part of the planning and sharing. This applies to those without children as well. If we can spend hours watching the television, we can at least give an hour to family sharing.

Remember that although money and possessions are important, being considerate of your marriage partner and his or her needs should be your number one priority. If each partner gives consideration to the needs of the other, then happiness will prevail. Consideration of only your own needs guarantees an unhappy household, as the needs of the other partner are secondary to your own. Selfishness doesn't make for a happy marriage.

*Over*

## *When married . . .*

Communication is necessary to convey your thoughts to each other. Never take it for granted that your wife or husband understands what's going on in your mind. Silence leads to an unhappy marriage, it leads to suspicion, unanswered questions, and a limited future.

Encourage your partner to have interests outside the family, be it volunteer work, a hobby, or something that allows them to use their special talents in a special way. This also allows for meeting new people and gives one not only a reason to get up in the morning, but the satisfaction of accomplishment.

Don't let having children come between you because you're giving so much time to the children. A mother who neglects her husband when raising children can bring about a loss of the former closeness between husband and wife. It's important to have a balance on the part of the woman in making her husband feel included in the parenting of the children. The children will benefit as well.

AND MOST IMPORTANT . . . Say "I love you" at least once each day. Love is the glue that binds the marriage into an ongoing relationship, year upon year upon year. No matter how old you become, we like to hear it said in a sincere and loving way, "I LOVE YOU."

# *About the Author*

Sidney J. Smith has been involved with human services for the past fifty-three years. He is the administrator of Non-Profits, Inc. in Santa Barbara, California, for which he serves as a consultant to human service organizations and encourages volunteerism within the community. His years as an active member of Kiwanis, an organization dedicated to community service, has provided him with a springboard to reach out to others in a very significant way. Smith established Keywanettes, the first Kiwanis-sponsored volunteer program for high school girls. He was responsible for developing one of the first two hospice programs in the United States. Through Non-Profits, Inc. he has assisted over three thousand individuals and agencies serving human service needs, qualifying him as knowledgeable in the field of human relations. His interests range from the very young to the elderly.

Smith has an honorary Doctor of Letters degree from Westmont College in Santa Barbara. He has received awards as the community's Man of the Year, the business community's Citizen of the Year, and the religious community's Layman of the Year.

Smith's greatest attribute for being qualified to write this book lies in his and his present wife's combined 108 years of successful marriage. It is his hope that this book will help to reduce the extremely high percentage of divorces that occur in today's world.

# *Appendix*

The associations listed below may be of help to anyone contemplating marriage. Many of them have branches throughout the United States or conduct seminars in major cities. To locate a program near you, contact the organization or see their Web site.

The Caring Couples Network (CCN)
c/o Family Ministries General Board of Discipleship
Box 840
Nashville, TN 37202

615-340-7170; http://www.discipleshipresources.org
CCN is an ecumenical ministry initiated by the General Board of Discipleship of the United Methodist Church. It arranges teams for mentoring, friendship, enrichment events, support, and other resources for engaged and marriage couples, parents, and couples and families in distress.

Catholic Engaged Encounter: Christian Marriage Preparation
Stan & Carol Isham, National Executive Team
800-811-3661; http://www.engaged-encounter.org

These nationwide retreat weekends are designed to give couples the opportunity to talk honestly and privately and share attitudes about ambitions, goals, money, sex, children, and family. Open to all Christian faiths.

Center for Relationship Development
Les and Leslie Parrott, Ph.D.s
Seattle, WA 98119

800-286-9333; http://www.realrelationships.com
The Center focuses on solving relationship problems before they begin. Books, tapes, curricula, and seminars are available nationwide for married couples and singles.

The Coalition for Marriage, Family and Couples Education, LLC
Diane Sollee, MSW, Director
53120 Belt Road, N.W.
Washington, D.C. 20015
202-362-3332; http://smartmarriages.com
The Coalition is dedicated to bringing information about marriage education courses to the public. Couples can learn the skills at any stage of relationship—dating, engaged, as newlyweds, or after many years of marriage.

Compassion Workshops: Anger & Violence Regulation
Steven Stosny, Ph.D.
16220 Frederick Road, Suite 404
Gaithersburg, MD 20877
301-921-2010; http://www.compassionpower.com
Educational programs for individuals, families, and organizations. Compassion for self and others creates individual growth, cooperation, and stronger emotional bonds, while decreasing guilt, shame, fear of abandonment, and the anger, resentment, abuse, and violence they cause.

Couple Communication Program
Sherod Miller, Ph.D.
Interpersonal Communication Programs, Inc.
7201 South Broadway
Littleton, CO 80122
800-328-5099; 303-794-1764;
http://www.couplecommunication.com
Learn eleven skills for effective talking, listening, and collaborative conflict resolution. This educational program is taught in groups or to individual couples privately.

The Couples School
Judith Coche, Ph.D.
The Coche Center/Academy House, #410
1420 Locust Street
Philadelphia, PA 19102
215-735-1908

This program is for every couple—married, engaged, or intimately partnered—who cares enough about their relationship to maintain and improve communication. Not psychotherapy or marriage counseling.

The Engaged Workshop
Marty and Roger Gilbert
20 Harstrom Place
Norwalk, CN 06853
203-838-2990

In this church-based program, engaged couples learn communication and conflict resolution skills while developing motivation and confidence to work through predictable struggles.

Gottman Institute
John Gottman, Ph.D.
Seattle, WA
888-523-9042

Founded by marriage research pioneer John Gottman, the Institute provides courses for marriage communication skills.

Life Innovations, Inc.
David Olson, Ph.D., Director
Box 190
Minneapolis, MN 55440
800-331-1661; 651-635–0511; http://www.lifeinnovation.com

The Prepare Program helps prepare couples for marriage. Couples first take an inventory with 195 questions and then attend three or four feedback sessions that focus on communication, conflict resolution, family of origin, finances, and goals.

Making Marriage Work (MMW)
Elana Rimmon Zimmerman, Director
Sylvia Weishaus, Ph.D., Clinical Director
University of Judaism
15600 Mulholland Drive
Los Angeles, CA 90077
310-440-1233

A premarital and marital training program for Jewish and interfaith couples.

Marriage Alive International, Inc.
Claudia & David Arp, MSSW
Box 31408
Knoxville, TN 37930-1408
888-690-6667; http://www.marriagealive.com

Marriage Alive offers national seminars and skill-based, practical resources (books, videos, and seminars) for all stages of marriage, engaged through empty nest.

Mars and Venus Institute
Mill Valley, CA
888-463-6684; http://www.mars-venus-counselors.com

Support groups and individual couples programs offer couples and/or singles the opportunity to immerse themselves in the principles of John Gray, Ph.D., author of *Men Are from Mars, Women Are from Venus* books.

National Institute of Relationship Enhancement
Bernard Guerney, Ph.D., Director
4400 East-West Highway
Bethesda, MD 20904
800-432-6454; 301-986-1479; http://www.nire.org

Couples learn skills to increase mutual understanding and emotional responsiveness, resolve conflicts and problems, and establish new patterns of personal and interactive behaviors. Weekend group or one-couple instruction can be scheduled.

Pairs for Life: Pairs for Love
Developed by Lori Gordon, Ph.D.
888-724-7748; http://www.pairs.com

Remove barriers to love and pleasure. Develop emotional literacy and live life the way it was meant to be, with love, passion, and deep fulfillment through semester, intensives, weekend, one-day, or evening preparation programs.

Partners
Lynne Gold-Bikin, J.D., Founder & director:
ABA Family Law Section
750 North Lake Shore Drive
Chicago, IL 60611
312-988-5603;
http://www.abanet.org/family/partners/home.html

The American Bar Association Section of Family Law, in conjunction with the PAIRS Foundation, has produced Partners, a marriage course for high school students.

PREP: The Prevention & Relationship Enhancement Program
Howard Markman, Ph.D., Scott Stanley, Ph.D., Directors
800-366-0166; http://members.aol.com/prepinc

Based on over twenty years of empirical research, PREP is a comprehensive premarital/marital program that teaches couples essential skills for maintaining a lasting love.

# Recommended Reading

Barnett, Doyle. *20 Advanced Communication Tips for Couples: A 90-Minute Investment in a Better Relationship* (Crown Publishing, 1997). This book seeks to challenge readers and offer them an opportunity for personal growth. Each tip is accessible with advice addressing such issues as being right or being fair, feelings before facts, and learning to be wrong.

Biehl, Bobb, and Cheryl Biehl. *Pre-Marriage Questions: Getting to "Really Know" Your Life-Mate-To-Be* (Broadman & Holman Publishers, 1996). In this booklet the authors have devised a list of questions for couples contemplating marriage to discuss prior to tying the knot. They also provide a step-by-step method for resolving disagreements before they threaten the relationship.

Engel, Marjorie. *Weddings: A Family Affair* (Wilshire Publications, 1998). This book presents the common problems and practical solutions of planning a wedding of a second marriage and a wedding for couples with divorced parents.

Gottman, John, and Nan Silver (Contributor). *Seven Principles for Making Marriage Work* (Crown Publishing, 1999). Gottman points out that there's more to a solid, emotionally intelligent marriage than sharing every feeling and thought. Just as Masters and Johnson were pioneers in the study of human sexuality, Dr. John Gottman has revolutionized the study of marriage.

_____. *Why Marriages Succeed or Fail: And How You Can Make Yours Last* (Fireside, 1995). Based on a study of more than two hundred marriages over a period of twenty years, a psychologist reveals new perspectives on marriage, shatters conventional wisdom, and presents practical exercises and guidelines.

Gray, John. *Mars and Venus on a Date : A Guide for Navigating the 5 Stages of Dating to Create a Loving and Lasting Relationship* (Harper Mass Market Paperbacks, 1998). Without fear or favor, *Mars and Venus on a Date* dissects the dynamics between men and women and the five stages each relationship must pass through: attraction, uncertainty, exclusivity, intimacy, and, finally, engagement (for marriage, of course).

_____. *Men Are From Mars, Women Are From Venus: A Practical Guide for Improving Communication and Getting What You Want in Your Relationships* (HarperCollins Publishers, 1992). Relationship counselor John Gray focuses on the differences between men and women and offers a simple solution: couples must acknowledge and accept these differences before they can develop happier relationships.

Hoffman, Jeffrey A. *Are We Compatible?: Questions for Couples* (Andrews McMeel Publishing, 1998). Before making the most important decision in your life, the author thinks you might want to read this book.

Littauer, Florence, and Fred Littauer. *After Every Wedding Comes a Marriage.* This upbeat guide to a lasting, harmonious marriage is filled with advice from the perspective of Florence Littauer and her husband, Fred. They offer valuable insights to nurture a loving union from newlyweds to golden anniversary veterans.

McDonough, Yona Zeldis, and Howard Yahm. *Between "Yes" and "I Do": Resolving Conflict and Anxiety During Your Engagement* (Citadel Press, 1998). This sensitive, insightful book offers invaluable advice to the couple that enables them to eliminate tension and make their engagement the happiest time of their lives.

Parrott, Les, and Leslie Parrott. *Getting Ready for the Wedding* (Zondervan Publishing House, 1998). The Parrotts, along with several well-known marriage experts, explore ten topics the wedding consultant can't help you with, including How do we know when we're ready for marriage? What's the secret to a great engagement? and After the honeymoon.

_____. *Saving Your Marriage Before It Starts: Seven Questions to Ask Before (and After You Marry)* (Zondervan Publishing House, 1995). Whether you're contemplating marriage, engaged, or newly married, Les and Leslie will lead you through the thorniest spots in establishing a relationship. You'll discover how to communicate, not just talk.

Phillips, Bob. *How Can I Be Sure?: Questions to Ask Before You Get Married* (Harvest House Publishers, 1999). Freshly updated to reflect the concerns of today, this workbook asks those considering marriage to respond to insightful questions about everything from their communication patterns to their future dreams.

Smalley, Gary. *Forever Love: 119 Ways to Keep Your Love Alive* (J. Countryman, 1998). This is a book of timeless principles that will have you falling in love with your partner all over again.

Smalley, Gary, and Norma Smalley. *It Takes Two to Tango: More Than 250 Secrets to Communication, Romance and Intimacy in Marriage* (Focus on the Family Publications, 1997). Highlighting Gary Smalley's greatest insights on what makes a marriage thrive, this collection of quotes features the perspectives of both him and his wife, Norma—wisdom that will help you create a lasting, loving relationship.

Stanley, Scott. *The Heart of Commitment* (Thomas Nelson Publishing, 1998). This book by the codirector of the Center for Marital and Family Studies at the University of Denver focuses on creating a commitment-based marriage.

Wallerstein, Judith S., et al. *The Good Marriage: How and Why Love Lasts* (Warner Books, 1996). This book charts the four general types of marriage—the romantic, the rescue, the companionate, and the traditional—and the nine tasks essential to forging a successful one, based on intimate interviews with fifty couples who consider themselves happy.

Wright, H. Norman and Wes Roberts. *Before You Say "I Do": A Marriage Preparation Manual for Couples* (Harvest House Publishers, 1997). Drawn from years of marriage preparation and enrichment seminars, this handbook delivers solid information on how you and your partner can make your marriage all that it is meant to be, particularly through incorporating Christ into your relationship.

# Send Us Your Questions

Is there an important question you feel was omitted in this book? If so, and you would like to submit one or more questions for inclusion in a future edition, we welcome your suggestions.

If we accept your question, we will acknowledge you in a list of contributors in the new edition and send you a complimentary copy of the book. (If we receive more than one question on the same subject, the first one received and used will be acknowledged.) Any additional comments you might wish to make are also welcome. We appreciate your interest and hope this book has helped you to better prepare for your wonderful journey ahead.

Please send your entries to:

Sidney James Publishing Company
115 East Mission Street
Santa Barbara, CA 93101

# Quick Order Form

Telephone orders:  Call 1-877-274-7500 toll free. Have your credit card ready.

Fax orders:  (805) 569-2787. Send this form.

E-mail orders:  orders@marriagequestions.com

Web site orders:  www.marriagequestions.com

Postal orders:  Sidney James Publishing Company
115 East Mission Street
Santa Barbara, CA 93101

I would like to order _____ copies of *Before Saying YES to Marriage . . . 101 Questions to Ask Yourself* @ $15.95 each

Name: _____

Address: _____

City: _____ Zip: _____

Telephone: _____ E-mail _____

Sales tax:  Please add 7.75% ($1.31 for each book) for books shipped to California addresses.

Shipping:  U.S.: $4.00 for the first book and $2.00 for each additional book.

International:  $9.00 for the first book and $5.00 for each additional book (estimate).

Payment:  ☐ Check   ☐ Visa   ☐ MasterCard

Card number: _____ Exp. date _____

Name on card: _____

Signature: _____

*THANK YOU FOR YOUR ORDER!*

# Quick Order Form

Telephone orders: Call 1-877-274-7500 toll free. Have your credit card ready.

Fax orders: (805) 569-2787. Send this form.

E-mail orders: orders@marriagequestions.com

Web site orders: www.marriagequestions.com

Postal orders: Sidney James Publishing Company
115 East Mission Street
Santa Barbara, CA 93101


I would like to order _____ copies of *Before Saying YES to Marriage . . . 101 Questions to Ask Yourself* @ $15.95 each

Name: _____

Address: _____

City: _____ Zip: _____

Telephone: _____ E-mail _____

Sales tax: Please add 7.75% ($1.31 for each book) for books shipped to California addresses.

Shipping: U.S.: $4.00 for the first book and $2.00 for each additional book.

International: $9.00 for the first book and $5.00 for each additional book (estimate).

Payment: ☐ Check   ☐ Visa   ☐ MasterCard

Card number: _____ Exp. date _____

Name on card: _____

Signature: _____

*THANK YOU FOR YOUR ORDER!*